TIMES OF OUR LIVES

Memories of the 20th Century

Compiled by
Sue Brown, Gordon Roxby and Neil Smith

Published in the United Kingdom 2014
by Roxby Publications

ISBN 978-0-9556232-9-5

Special Note from the Publishers:
Any surplus from the sales of this book will be donated to
St. Luke's (Cheshire) Hospice

Introduction:

Humanity's greatest leap; the improvement in our living conditions in the 80-year span between the 1930s and the 2010s is almost immeasurable. The many contributors to this book lived through those momentous years.

Take housing. How far removed are we today from those back-to-back slums with only cold–running water and their unforgettable freezing outside toilets, or from those large families, perhaps with six or seven children, forced to share two cramped bedrooms between them?

Cooking has gone from coal-fired ranges in the living room to gas and electric cookers in bright modern kitchens. Domestic heating, unheard of on upper floors, once meant a coal fire in one room, laboriously lit each day. Now, it's touch-of-a-button central heating throughout the house with electric lighting instead of paraffin lamps and gas lights. Floorings of warm fitted carpets and a multitude of easy-to-clean hard wearing floors have replaced cold lino and rough rag rugs.

Think about how washday was a marathon five-day routine; lighting fires under 'coppers' in wash houses, struggling with mangles to squeeze out the water, hanging the clothes to dry on long lines then ironing with heavy implements that had to be heated on the range. Now, of course, washing machines, tumble driers and lightweight steam irons cut the chore drastically.

Home entertainment was communal in those bygone days. Families played board games together and their children's playground was the street. Remember how we gathered around bulky valve radios to hear our favourite programmes? Television eventually appeared, of course, but in black and white and on tiny screens that, rightly, seem so primitive to today's big-screen offerings.

Communications have become almost mind-boggling, leaping from a telephone 'at the bottom of the stairs' (in the few fortunate homes that had one) to mobile phones where the world is at people's fingertips. Access to knowledge was limited to books or papers from reference libraries. Now, thanks to computers and their ilk, we can access such knowledge in seconds.

Education has made giant strides, too. Those at university and in further education have risen from around just five per cent of 18 year olds to many times that figure. Perhaps one of our greatest advances has been in women's rights. Who would have thought that, once upon a time, some women were automatically sacked from their job if they got married or became pregnant?

Transport by car, once the preserve of the elite in the 1940s, is now widely accessible. International air and sea travel, almost unheard of for the ordinary man and woman, is these days as common as catching a bus was back then. Great advances in science and engineering means we can often holiday abroad cheaper than in Britain. And we get more leisure time to take them, too, with annual holidays extended from two weeks a year to five or six.

Our improvements in living conditions include better health. Effective medicine became available from the 1940s. Life expectancy then was 63 for men and 68 for women. In 2014 it is 85 for men and 89 for women - back in 1841, it was 40 and 42 respectively!

These, and many other advances, mean that most people in the United Kingdom today live longer and healthier lives than kings and queens of two centuries ago.

Here, then, are the stories of the Crewe and Nantwich U3A local history members who have lived through this largest leap in human history.

Gordon Roxby 2014

Acknowledgements

Thanks go to the contributors for their stories. They are mostly from the Local History One Group of Crewe and Nantwich U3A (University of the Third Age) with some contributions from other member groups. Thanks also go to the Book Project Committee of Sue Brown, Gordon Roxby and Neil Smith for managing the contributions and arrangements over two years. In addition special thanks go to Roy David and Greta Guest for their professional editing of the material and to *liverpoolpicturebook.com* for the use of some of their extensive library and to Ken Rogers, author of *The Lost Tribe of Everton*. We also appreciate the help given by our printers Printdomain.

Cover design by Mediascope, Scarborough.

Printed by Printdomain

Note: for more details about the U3A, please see last page.

MEMORIES OF A WAR BABY

by Anon

My mother was German and in the years just before the Second World War, life was very difficult living in the slums of London. Although she spoke very good English, she was a shy person. Consequently, the neighbours would not have anything to do with her. When my sister (1934) and later myself (1936) were due to be born, there were no relatives in England to help in a home birth as my father was a Scot with his family in Glasgow and America. Although we had a flat with electricity and running water, Mum had to go into the local workhouse for her confinement. She was not allowed to give birth in hospital as there were no complications. She returned to our flat as soon as she was able and we continued to live there until I was 18 years old.

But my sister and I only discovered in 2011 (aged 75 and 77) the fact we were born in such circumstances. Mum was so ashamed of going into a workhouse that she never told us and it remained a secret with her to her death at the age of 95. You see, as soon as the war started, the workhouse was turned into a local hospital and so we always assumed that we had been born in this hospital. Over the years I often wondered why we had a normal-looking address on our birth certificates instead of the name of the hospital. It was not until my niece was studying our family tree that she found out the significance of the address - it was the old workhouse, now the local hospital. Of course, it was less of a stigma than having the workhouse name on the certificate.

The war started when I was three years old and by this time my father could no longer live with what he considered the shame of my mother being German, so he left us (they had married in the US in 1932). Mum had no option but to go out to work to support us. She was made to do essential war work at the local laundry, sterilising Free French Army uniforms, while my sister and I took ourselves to school, doing jobs in the house till Mum came home at 6pm.

7

While my sister and I were at home during the day, we had to promise to go into the air raid shelter if the siren went off. But as soon as the raid was over, we were out to see what buildings had been damaged and watch wardens from the ARP (Air Raid Precautions) and firemen digging in the bombed buildings to try to release anyone buried in the rubble. We had no concept of the finality of death and didn't turn a hair seeing bodies brought out.

We did not go into the shelter with our neighbours when Mum was at home, but stayed in our ground floor flat where my sister and I would sit under the table. At night the three of us would cuddle up together in a double bed and listen to Mum telling us stories until the 'all-clear' siren sounded. One thing I found strangely reassuring during these air raids was Mum telling us that if a bomb had our names on it, then we would all go together. We spent many winter nights all cuddled up together in this bed, listening to these stories even when there was no money to pay for light or coal. What was not so nice was when we were so hungry that we cried ourselves to sleep!

Let me tell you about our 'Home Sweet Home.' The flat left much to be desired and had been condemned long before the war started. Property was in such short supply that you had to be grateful for what you could get. We had gas, electricity and cold running water. The problem was that the tap was not the only supply of water. The main room had rising damp which meant the walls were constantly wet when it rained. The floor in this room was also badly affected and mum would make regular visits to the Health Inspector to try to persuade the landlord to replace the rotten floorboards which often gave way as we walked about. We learned at a young age to walk only over the joists or we faced going through the floor and getting some very painful cuts and scratches on our legs. Fortunately we never broke any bones.

The flat was also overrun with mice. This did not bother me as they were my means of getting even with my sister. Being the eldest, she was always 'in charge' and bossed me about all the time. She hated mice and so when I had as much as I could take, I would pick one up by its tail and chase her round the streets with it until I felt that we were even. She always got her own back as Mum would be told as soon as she got home from work and I got spanked with a wooden hairbrush so that I could not sit down for the rest of the evening - but it was worth it.

Another problem with the flat was that it was joined to the high wall at the back of the yards belonging to the local shops. All the neighbourhood cats seemed to collect on the top of this wall and wail all night. It sounded to us like babies crying and no matter how Mum tried to explain, we were convinced it was babies wanting their mummies. To get to the top of the wall, cats used our bedroom windowsill as a half-way stage. It had been boarded up and these hungry cats would sit on our sill and scratch the board to be let in. My sister and I thought it might be robbers trying to get into our bedroom − not that we had anything worth stealing! In fact, there were so many stray cats around that people said that the less-reputable butchers skinned them and sold them as rabbits (which were not rationed).

Most children were evacuated many times during the war − as were we (five times in all). Mum came with us the first time to Sevenoaks and we had hardly arrived when my sister became very ill. If it had not been for the fact that the daughter of the house was a nurse, who diagnosed a perforated appendix and took her straight to the hospital, my sister would have died.

Next, we went to Cornwall to stay at the local forge. That didn't last long because I badly burned my hand, so we were taken back to London. Then it was to Wokingham, Berkshire, where we had three different homes, all of which could not have been more different.

The first home was spotless, but the owners did not realise that children of four and six would sometimes get a bit grubby after a day at school. This ended with a bizarre form of punishment which has affected me ever since. Regardless of which one of us had got their dress dirty, the grandmother would pop out her glass eye into her open hand and we would each have to stroke it! By the time mum came down to see us, I was terrified of making any sudden movement in case my eyes fell out. And, to this day, I cannot bare anything to do with eyes. Even when my children were small and perhaps got a bit of grit in their eyes, I would have to ask a neighbour to deal with it. Personally, I would prefer to go to the dentist a dozen times than once to any optician. I dread to think what will happen if I ever have to have any form of eye treatment!

So we moved again when Mum found out about the grandmother's cruel mode of chastisement. Thus, we moved on to our second home in Wokingham - the exact opposite of the first. The house was very poorly furnished and untidy with seven children in the household. They all wore hand-me-down clothes from older siblings, all of which had seen better days. Although we ourselves were very poor, Mum would sometimes buy 6d remnants of cloth from our local market and make us pretty dresses. Old jumpers could be unpicked as well and two new ones knitted out of three old ones. We had both been taught to knit to occupy our time sitting under the table during the air raids with the result that we were both well dressed. One day, Mum had hardly gone out of the door after bringing us a new dress each when the woman began dressing her girls in our clothes and making us wear their old threadbare ones. Fortunately, it was not long before Mum was down to visit us again and was cross to see other children wearing clothes she had made.

Our third home in Wokingham was exactly the opposite of the first two. In fact, we thought that we had died and gone to heaven! Mr and Mrs Francis were the 'grandparents' we had never known. They never had any children of their own, yet they loved and cared for us as if we were their grandchildren. A great friendship blossomed and we visited them many times. Years later they even gave both my sister and I away at our respective weddings. Back in London, we soon got into the habit of getting ourselves off to school and then doing jobs until Mum came home from work. We took it in turns to prepare the potatoes and vegetables, while the other cleared out and laid the fire. We were under strict instruction not to do any cooking or to light the fire as we were still only five and seven years old. We also had to take the 'bagwash' to the nearby laundry, then collect it on our way home from school. That was a bit of a struggle for us as when it was wet and very heavy.

We did not mind all the household chores because we knew that if everything got done by Friday, we were guaranteed an exciting weekend. Mum would take us out all over the area; to the West End to window-shop along Oxford Street and Regents Street, to the many

10

big museums or parks if the weather was good. We walked all over the place, taking a bottle of water and some bread with margarine and sugar with us as a picnic at some exciting spot. If it was too wet for us to go out she would always find something interesting for us to do - even if it was only sliding around on our bottoms on an old rag to polish the lino on our bedroom floor. We had a very poor childhood but we certainly never considered ourselves underprivileged, the key to it being that we were so desperately loved.

A highlight memory of after the war was when we sat for hours outside Buckingham Palace when Prince Charles was born on my sisters 14th birthday. Prince Philip came out of the Palace after visiting the King and Queen. His car stopped at the gate and he told our group of people waiting there: 'Mother and baby are both doing well.' It was very exciting to be spoken to by Royalty for a kid from the slums! We were also at the gate again at the Queen's Coronation. In fact, very little went on in London that we did not see – providing it was free, of course. Mother took us everywhere.

Children living in London in the 1940s had a much disrupted school life, leaving whatever they were doing to march down to the air raid shelter whenever the siren sounded. Most were evacuated several times and therefore went to different schools. These became overcrowded so that lessons were often taken in the hall with one class in each corner. Schools were bombed, too, as was the second school I attended. Fortunately it occurred at night so no children were hurt, but it obviously caused a lot of inconvenience.

During my primary education, I attended six different schools and my sister, seven. I passed my 11-plus and was offered a place in a private school which my mother was thrilled about. For the first time since she had come to London, she had something to be proud about instead of being looked down upon. I had always enjoyed school and at this one, nobody apart from the staff knew that my mother was German and so I could start on an even keel, although I must say that the girls there did not seem to have the same biased views as the folk where I lived. I had to have a rather posh uniform which included a straw Panama hat in summer and a navy velour hat in winter. Trouble was, I stuck out like a sore thumb in the area around my home and was often taunted. My sister had gone to the local secondary school and had been absorbed into the crowd, but my school and uniform made me different.

Another girl from near my home also passed the exam, although she went to a different grammar school. She, too, was then ostracised for being different, but at long last it meant I had a best friend. In the inner areas of London in the 1940s there was a very strong community spirit among the locals although they did not readily assimilate folk who were in any way different. I loved school but it was almost as difficult as at home because I still did not fit in. I could not join in with all the extra-curricular activities as we did not have the money to pay for them.

I suppose the fact that our father left us meant that our Mum was quite possessive with us. When my sister was 19, she had to go searching for our father and persuade him to sign his consent for her to get married as Mum would not give it, even though my sister's young man was a very nice reliable lad with a good job.

When my turn came, she was even more adamant because it would have left her on her own. To placate her, we agreed that we would not get married until we had bought a house of our own. Just two years later, however, Mother was horrified when we announced we had got our deposit, saving like mad. I suppose it was natural to feel guilty about 'leaving' Mum after all she had done for us and the wartime experiences which drew us all closer.

But here was when fate took a hand. Mum was, by now, a supervisor for a pharmaceutical company, having worked her way up within the company and they just so happened to be expanding to a new factory in Welwyn Garden City. Companies in these satellite towns were allocated brand new housing for their key workers to ease London's housing problems. Consequently, she was offered a brand new flat surrounded by grass, trees and glorious open spaces.

This was the answer to my problem! We were finally given her blessing on our marriage (even though I was already 21) and bought an old terraced house which we began to do up. And so Mum was pleased to move to her brand new flat in Welwyn Garden City to enjoy her new surroundings along with the many friends she had made at work.

ON CRUSADE WITH BILLY GRAHAM

by Anon

I was born and brought up in London and, at the age of three, I was sent to Sunday school with my five year old sister to the local Shaftesbury Mission. I stayed attending the various meetings there until it closed due to lack of support in 1951 when I was 15. During this time I was given a firm grounding in the gospel and also enjoyed the mid-week activities. There was a Girls' Life Brigade group where we worked for badges to sew on the sleeves of our uniforms, played games and did gymnastics on an old vaulting horse which to me was the highlight of the evening. Later, this was disbanded and a youth club was set up instead which was less formal but still good fun and kept the local children off the streets for one night a week.

After the mission closed it was quickly demolished and a block of much needed flats were built on the site. It had originally been built as a soup kitchen for 'The Ragged School Union', so it was a piece of our history lost forever. My only sad memory came at the Christmas party when I was about six years old. The war was still on, of course, so a party was a real treat. I was thoroughly enjoying it all and looking forward to the prize-giving for good attendance at Sunday school during the year. My sister and I always had the highest scores, so I was expecting a nice prize which would have been a real luxury for us.

The prizes were second-hand items, handed in to the Shaftesbury Society to be distributed to poorer children. But some of them were in perfect condition and were considered great treasures. I watched with bated breath while the Superintendent started giving out the best presents, working down to the more shabby items to the children who did not attend the Mission but only came in for the party.

As I watched the last present given away I could contain myself no longer and burst into tears. It was only then that they realised I had been forgotten - despite having the best attendance. They gathered up all the bits and pieces which they had discarded as rubbish and, with an apology, handed them over. I have to say I was devastated as this was my main present of the year! After Kimpton Mission closed, I went to another Shaftesbury Mission at Waterloo where the gospel was faithfully preached each Sunday evening. But apart from helping with the Sunday school in the afternoon, there were no other meetings in the week and no one of my own age to talk to.

In March the next year, the father of a girl in my class at school was taking a group of his parishioners to White City to hear the American evangelist, Billy Graham, and she offered me one of the spare places. Thousands of people went to these crusades each evening to hear him speak of God and how Jesus Christ is our only way to Heaven through His death for the forgiveness of our sins. At the end of these meetings, large numbers of the congregation went forward to accept Jesus as their Saviour, myself included. These campaigns were held at Wembley and other large sporting venues in London for several years and later extending to other large towns around the country. Despite all these crusades, the congregations at my mission continued to fall.

Later, I met my future husband and he also attended a Shaftesbury Mission, but his was at London Bridge. We tried to support both missions but numbers at mine continued to fall and eventually had to close in 1958. It had been set up by a group of professional men who called it 'Working Men's Mission'. After closure it became a hostel for men living rough on the Thames Embankment where they could have the Bible explained to them. After a meal they would be given a bed for the night.

We continued to attend Arthur's Mission at London Bridge, being married by the Superintendent (our insurance agent) at Bermondsey Gospel Mission. In the 1950s, only churches and a few smaller religious buildings were allowed to conduct marriage services and if the person conducting it was not a recognised minister then the local Registrar of the borough had to attend to witness it. There was no getting married at the local hotel or beauty spot in those days! At that time there was a group of about 20 young people at the mission, but as we all married and gradually moved away from the area, only the very elderly were left and so this mission also closed in 1973.

The concept of the extended family was being eroded by companies moving out of London and young families needing to live where they could find work.

We moved up to Cheshire in 1969 and the next day we had a visit from the local vicar to welcome us to the area. When he heard we were regular churchgoers, he tried to persuade us to go to his church. Two hours and many cups of tea later without any success, he told us that Wheelock Heath Baptist Church might suit us. We started to attend there and it soon became our spiritual home. In contrast to all the other churches I have attended, this one has a growing congregation; from 40 to 50 at the morning service in 1969 until now when we have the service in the local high school as we have outgrown our own church building.

PLAYING FOR A 'PEA SHILLING TOOSE'

by Jill Ashley

I was one of five children and we lived in an avenue of houses surrounded by fields in Tarporley. The lanes and meadows became our playground, so it was certainly a rural childhood. I have vivid memories of the hay-making and the cutting of the corn. With the latter, several local men would shoot the rabbits as they were forced out of their diminishing cover. The men would each go home carrying one or two for supper and with several more to sell!

The local hunt was a common and picturesque scene, but we were not allowed to fraternise with them as Dad (and an older brother) strongly disapproved of the 'sport.' Years later as an adult, I remember my brother Colin, driving home from Chester and spotting the hunt in full pursuit. He saw the fox dive into an underground culvert. Knowing the exact location of the manhole where the hunt would want to send the hounds down, he drove straight to it, stopped firmly over it, and refused to move. The hunt members were furious with him banging on his car windows and cursing him, but he wouldn't budge till they got fed up and rode away.

Aged five, our youngest sister contracted a TB hip and had to go into an orthopaedic hospital near Oswestry. She was there for five long years - four of them being flat on her back on a frame specially designed for the purpose. I remember a lot of talk among the adults at the time was whether our provider's milk had been pasteurised – this would be 1945. At some point after that, I remember seeing the vehicles of the various milk suppliers now carrying the prominent information: 'Tuberculin Tested.'

During the war, I remember spending much of one Christmas Eve under the stairs when an air raid started – something that caused me great consternation. I was unperturbed about any bombs, however, but in case Santa Claus was confused by all the noise and commotion and failed to leave us any presents! Dad was in the Home Guard and

I remember the sinister look of his rifle and bayonet hanging in the hall.

My father was a marvellous man. In his younger years he was a farm worker, quite politically minded and a member of the Labour Party and the Agricultural Workers' Union. They had a difficult time getting the union established, the farmers being equally keen not to see it happen. With one child at that stage, the family lived in a tied cottage. The farmer for whom Dad worked, was a nasty man and the family was eventually evicted on trumped-up accusations. But really, it was because Dad wouldn't give up either his politics or his union activities. What wouldn't have helped his case, however, was the fact that one Bank Holiday Monday, while the farmer was at market, he had pasted glaring 'VOTE LABOUR' leaflets on the backs of all the cows!

We were pretty hard up, of course, but the large family next door were even more so. Dad recalled them continually roaming the fields looking for edible plants, nuts and fruits. That was a time when many people gathered mushrooms and blackberries to boost their food store and, when possible, sell to the local pubs and hotels.

We all went to the National C of E School, but I failed the 11-plus twice and was deeply disappointed. I was positively burning to get to the grammar school as my brother had already done. I was top of the class at the end of every term, and was fully expected to pass. I had very little facility with numbers and so mathematics was almost closed to me - even the simple basics terrified me. It wouldn't have been so bad if there had been a secondary school I could have gone to, but no, you stayed at the same elementary school and learned very little more after the age of 11. Fortunately, when I reached the age of 15, the opening of a further education college in Chester provided an opportunity for enhancement. I enrolled for a comprehensive two-year course, which included secretarial skills, and came away with good exam results and a bunch of certificates. This promptly led to a job with a business company and I rose through the ranks very happily.

When I was aged about nine, my eldest sister who was in the ATS stationed in Germany, came home on leave and brought me a very good Hohner harmonica. I'd had a cheaper harmonica for some time,

17

but this had a greater range and a superior sound. I was enthralled by the notes I could muster and would slope off somewhere quiet to practise. It was not long before I was merrily churning out every tune I knew and the harmonica accompanied me everywhere I went.

One day I was playing it in the High Street on the way to school, completely lost in my own little world. Hearing a bit of a commotion, I looked up and found a group of American soldiers leaning out of the windows of the Swan Hotel across the road. I stopped and gazed up at them and saw they were clapping and calling out to me. I've realised since that they were probably delighted with this little snippet of English life. I, though, was a little embarrassed and when they started throwing down chewing gum, I didn't know whether to be glad or sorry. They shouted to me to pick it up, which I eventually did. It was even more of a shock and embarrassment when they next threw down a two shilling piece - a 'pea shilling toose' as my brother would say, being very much into Spoonerisms at the time! Next thing I knew, one of the soldiers had come down into the street, picked up the coin and pressed it firmly into my hand.

The avenue where we lived was on a quiet country road and the American soldiers billeted in the village were often brought there to drill. We kids idolised them although we reckoned their marching was not a patch on the British. Why we considered ourselves any kind of judge of such matters I can't imagine! Twice, Dad brought an American soldier home from the local pub and they became like members of the family, corresponding for many years afterwards, both from Europe and when they were back home.

Sometime in the 1940s, a collection of prefabs were hastily erected on the site of the old Tarporley Racecourse and this caused quite a stir. It was some time before the reason for it became clear and, until then, the village was knee deep in speculation and rumour. Eventually they learned that it was to be a Prisoner of War camp for German and Italian soldiers. Aghast, some people feared they would slit the villagers' throats in their sleep, others that it was a scandal giving them our precious rations and the village buzzed with all sorts of speculation. In the end, though, I think calm was restored and most people realised the POWs were very decent blokes and

18

homesick for their own country. I remember a day when I was taking next door's twin babies for a walk in their pram and we came upon a couple of the German inmates taking a stroll. They seemed pleased to meet one of the natives and made a fuss of the babies. They tried hard to converse and one of them mentioned that the German word for twins was 'twirling.' For years, that's how I remembered it. Looking it up now, however, suggests the word was more likely 'Zwillinge,' so I think I got it wrong. But this encounter is still very vivid in my memory and is recalled with warmth.

The POWs eventually discovered the Saturday Night Dance at the village hall and apparently several romances blossomed, leading to marriage, children, and permanent residence over here. I haven't heard tell of any of the Americans billeted in the village marrying local girls, but maybe they were not here for very long. There are many gaps in my memory and knowledge of those years.

Many evacuees also arrived in Tarporley. I don't remember them but have heard accounts about it. We weren't required to house any as we had five children already. Dad did help with the organisation of it all the day they arrived, and when he came home for lunch he told Mum about the scruffy, very thin little boy who no one wanted. Promptly, Mum told Dad to go and get him. So Billy, as he was called, was brought home and the first thing Mum did was put him in the bath. He was found to be a quite adorable little boy and he looked at the food with amazement, particularly the traditional Sunday lunch. He didn't know the name of anything on his plate. He could only point to what he wanted as a second helping.

One of the amazing things about our dear Dad was that no one, including his family, could understand his vast general knowledge or the fact that he was so 'well read.' He'd had very little education, therefore limited access to books, or even libraries. But his vocabulary alone, amazed people, and his sense of humour was legendary.

This was all the more surprising when we considered he'd been taken out of school at the age of 10 and put to work on a farm. He was never bitter about that in spite of his craving for learning. He understood too well the need for every member of the family to work hard for their daily bread. Times were very hard indeed and,

19

thankfully, we've known nothing like it, (except, perhaps, second hand, in books or films). Various notables in the vicinity were very keen to have Dad's company, simply for his conversation. In his 60s he was in hospital for a hernia operation and a very 'well-to-do' man he didn't previously know was also in there at the same time. He was enthralled by Dad's company and, for years afterwards, he would call on Dad in the evening and take him to one of the many pubs in the area, purely for the rewarding nature of his conversation.

Our Mum was the most motherly mum imaginable, though nobody's fool and anyone putting a foot wrong would be firmly dealt with. Very sadly, she went down with cancer while I was expecting my first baby, about which she was so thrilled. At least she did live to see her granddaughter born, but it was very hard to accept that she should be taken when she'd meant so much to so many, not least, of course, to Dad.

After finishing with farming, Dad had various factory jobs, mostly light work, but he hated it and being indoors all day. His last job, though, was his favourite; as gardener in Tarporley Churchyard. He did all kinds of jobs, fixing and mending things as well as grafting trees and shrubs. Each succeeding Rector thought so much of him and would seek his counsel whatever the issue. He was in that job until he retired and led a more leisurely life (by his standards) tending his own garden and allotment in which he grew and sold many vegetables and fruit. Better parents than they, no one ever had!

OH NO, NOT THAT MICKEY MOUSE

by Elaine Attwater

I have a terrible early memory in the first years of the Second World War – all because of Mickey Mouse! You see, every household had been issued with gas masks because of the fear that the Germans would use toxic gas on the civilian population. In an effort to get me used to wearing my child's gas mask, my parents wanted a few 'trial runs.'

My mask was yellow and black and decorated with pictures of Mickey Mouse. It would be brought out to practise, accompanied by my parents' encouraging refrain: 'Here's your LOVELY Mickey Mouse mask.' I can still remember the terror, the screaming and the feeling of suffocation as it was clamped over my face. And, all the while, I could hear my mother's voice at first anguished, then angry: 'But it's a Mickey Mouse mask!'

Another unhappy experience was of an overnight stay (probably my only one) in the early 1940s at my paternal grandmother's home. She lived in a two-up, two-down terraced cottage in a Lancashire mill town, where she had been a cotton mill worker all her life. Like so many other homes at that time, it had no bathroom, just the one cold water tap in the kitchen and the lavatory was outside, down the yard, and shared with others. Grandma's life was poverty-stricken with no money for anything but absolute necessities.

Thus, when the time came for bed, I was laid down in a bed with no sheets. The feeling of being pricked and irritated by the coarse blankets next to be skin meant trying to get to sleep was extremely difficult. Too small to understand where the discomfort came from, I cried and cried. My mother soon realised what the problem was - but there were simply no sheets in the house. My beloved father, very unusually, showed his anger and shame to me and gave me a talking to. Perhaps that's what eventually shut me up.

In 1944, when I was seven, a young American airman came into my family's life. Cleve was stationed at the vast American air base at

21

Burtonwood, near Warrington. He had been invited to our home in the suburbs of Chester as a small act of hospitality on our part. Cleve repaid us many times over with huge American generosity. He would turn up with cigarettes in boxes of a thousand - American Camel and Lucky Strike. Once he even came with a parachute (I hate to think how he got it). For weeks afterwards, this vast swathe of parachute material quite literally filled our front room with mother and her sewing machine in its midst. Gradually, its size was reduced as various garments appeared, including a wonderful billowing nightdress for me.

On another very happy memorable day, Cleve arrived with two bananas – one for my elder brother, one for me. There I was, aged seven, and had never ever seen a banana before. I watched in the kitchen as my older brother peeled his banana, put it into a bowl and mashed it up with a fork. Then, he poured the top of the milk over it (that used to be the creamy part, in the days before milk was homogenised). But that wasn't for me. I wanted to take my banana outside to share with my friends. They, too, had never seen a banana before. I remember the occasion clearly. It was tea time on a hot summer's day. Soon the banana and I were surrounded by children and my friends took turns to have a bite. Even when only the skin was left, we scraped the inside with our thumb nails for every last little bit of that foreign fruit. A magical day!

TO LAUGH OR TO CRY

by Florence Bates

I was born at Linden Grange Maternity Home in Hungerford Avenue, Crewe, on 1st July 1943. I have lived at 165 Westminster Street all my life. My mum's name was Sarah May Chesworth and my dad's name was Clifford. I was the youngest in a family that included two brothers, William August and Brian William, both named after their grandad. I also had a sister named Barbara. My mother came from Burnley and was a weaver by trade. She had twelve looms to look after. She and Dad met on holiday in Blackpool.

My dad worked in Crewe Works, making axles for the engines' wheels. He was there for 49 years. After he retired, he continued with his hobby of fishing, winning many fishing matches. He used to cycle to the matches all over the district. My eldest brother, Bill enjoyed fishing, too, and won a lot of prizes, including the Cheshire Cup. He married his wife, Brenda, in 1953, and was then serving in Korea until the Peace Treaty was signed. He had three sons. Jonathan and Jeremy joined their dad and granddad in Crewe Works. The youngest son, Adrian, trained as a shunter and when the Royal Family came through Crewe in the Royal Train, he was called upon to move the trains as required. Bill died in 1980 and his wife Brenda died in 1977.

My brothers and sister all looked after me and took me to the pictures, the park and various other places. Brian took me to the Palace Cinema in Rosegrove, Burnley. He told my mum that I'd laughed when it was serious and cried when it was a comedy! When I was five I went to Edleston Road Infant School until I was eleven. My treat on a Saturday came via sweet coupons as we were still on rationing. I remember my Uncle Bill, my mother's brother, making me a dolls' house.

When I left Edleston Road School, I went to Bedford Street Secondary Modern School. When that closed, I went to the new

23

school called Kingsway Secondary Modern until I was 16. Then I went to Totties Hall College to train as a cook. While I was studying there I went to Switzerland with other students. It was the first time I had been abroad and we had a wonderful time.

I've had a long and varied career in the catering industry, from diet cook at the Barony Hospital at Nantwich to local nursing homes – even a remand home. The latter was the Redsands Remand Home on the Crewe Road at Willaston. The home was divided into three houses. The lads would sometimes abscond and the House Fathers used to go looking for them across the field. During the time of the electricity power cuts, one of the lads pinched a knife and threatened me. I ran after him to warn the House Father that the lad threatened to stab one of the other boys. From there I went as assistant catering officer at South Cheshire College on Dane Bank Avenue. Then I was appointed manager and worked there for 25 years. I dread to think how many meals, cakes, Christmas puddings and the like that I've made in my time. It must be millions!

SOLVING A COSTUME DRAMA

by Margaret Boschi

My most abiding happy memories are of our annual Sunday school pantomimes, written and directed by a teacher, Harold Swann, just after the war. The scripts were contemporary, set in the locality and included popular songs which we sang with so much energy and enjoyment. I must have been 15 when I played the part of Prince Charming in *Cinderella*. My younger sister also took part and in the following years we performed in many of the traditional pantos; the likes of *Jack and the Beanstalk* and *Dick Whittington* (my much younger brother played the part of the cat!).

There must have been a cast of around 40, children, teenagers, and adults. We all loved it and had so much fun. What struck me most of all was the amazing enthusiasm shown by both young and old during these productions. The war had not long finished and rationing was still in force. That could have posed quite a problem for our costume 'department.' But, fortunately, help was close at hand.

Dad just happened to be a manager with a local surgical dressing company. He was able to acquire quite a large amount of calico material. Now, this is where the wonderful team of mothers went into action. The material was cut, dyed into various colours and then taken by the mums into one of the Sunday school rooms where they set to work with their needles and threads – eventually emerging from their weekly meetings with a wonderful array of bright and colourful costumes.

What laughs we had in these performance! Two men playing the cow in *Jack and the Beanstalk* had everyone in stitches when the chap in the back half of the cow managed to slip over the edge of the stage.

I was the only other person on stage at the time so I rushed forward and tried to pull the cow back up. It was an absolute hoot and the audience laughed and clapped so much. There were probably

25

some people in the audience who thought it was all part of the act! Fortunately, no one was hurt and it was even suggested that we should keep the incident in for each performance – not that we did, mind.

Another occasion when things didn't go according to plan was when the Demon had to give me a gentle push. Well, he pushed a little too hard one night and I lost my balance and fell over, grazing my ankle bone quite badly. When I looked down, all I could see was the blood oozing out. Adapting that famous showbiz motto that 'the show must go on,' I quickly got up and tried to carry on as best I could. Fortunately I was due to 'exit left' quite quickly and I got the injury tended to.

I think my love of drama and theatre started during those happy days and I have been lucky enough to be involved for many years as an amateur. It also inspired me 20 years ago to join with a friend in forming a youth drama group where I hoped children would have the same bundle of fun and experiences that I'd had all those years ago.

A DATE WITH DESTINY

by Martin Bourne

Once upon a time, a packet of fags and a newspaper cost me my lifetime's 'freedom'. Sixty years ago, June 27, 1953, I walked out through the gates at Reaseheath for what I thought was the last time. How wrong I was. Reaseheath was a very different place to the fine establishment we know today. Then known as the Cheshire School of Agriculture, there were about 48 students; 31 male and 17 female, all of us aged between 17 and 22. We were all residential; our home was the men's hostel in Reaseheath Hall itself while the girls occupied the women's hostel, now known as Windsor Hall. We had a radio in the student's common room permanently tuned to radio Luxembourg, but no television.

The farming seemed to be pre-historic to many of us. Muck spreading was carried out with forks, spreading from heaps placed in rows along the field by a man with a horse and cart. There were two tractors at Hall Farm, but much of the work was still done by horses. The cows were all milked in the shippon, the milk then being carried across the yard to the dairy by students. All hedge cutting was, of course, by hand, mostly with dubbing shears so that they looked so well-manicured. The farm bailiff used to emphasise the fact that: 'We are in the public eye you know.'

When I left, there was talk of a student's reunion at the end of September. I wasn't really interested although when the day arrived, it was my weekend off so I decided to go. I enjoyed myself with my old friends, eventually gravitating to the Red Lion where a good few drinks were consumed before we returned to Reaseheath for a dance (discos had not yet been 'invented').

I returned to the reunion the following year, 1954, and turned up again the following year even though it now seemed a long time since I'd left. Up till five o'clock, there wasn't one of our year there, so I decided to call it a day and go home to Audlem. I stopped at Blackburn's paper shop in Pillory Street on the way home, desperate

27

to buy a packet of cigarettes. I also bought a newspaper, attracted by a headline, and then decided I'd return to Reaseheath to read it in the student's common room and have a smoke. Suddenly, three more ex-students from my year arrived so naturally, once again on the dot of opening time, we traipsed off to the Red Lion.

I was enjoying myself so much that, pretty soon, I became quite tipsy, to such an extent that the licensee became concerned about me driving my car. Now, it just so happened that there was a chatty bird on the next table who was proudly informing everyone that she'd passed her driving test the day before. Not many young ladies had a full licence in those days. The outcome was that the landlord asked the girl, whose name was Audrey, whether she would drive my car back up to Reaseheath. 'That's easy,' she said. 'I've even driven through the middle of Chester!'

So she got into the driving seat and I took the passenger side, while countless other inebriates piled onto the back. The next question was: 'Where's the gear stick?' It transpired she'd only driven a car with the gear stick on the steering column. So she worked the pedals and steering wheel and I operated the gear change. It was a memorable comedy of errors, but we arrived safely and during the later evening when I'd sobered up enough, I drove Audrey home. I asked her for a date to which she agreed (after first telling me that she was already engaged). From then on, things happened quickly and, eleven months on, we got married at Worleston Church.

Fifty seven years later, we are still married – and that's how a packet of cigarettes and a newspaper changed my life.

IN THE RED CORNER, WEIGHING JUST 2LBS

by Sue Brown

I was born on the 31st January at my Godmother's house in Watford. My expected date of arrival was the first of April. I weighed just 2lb and was, therefore, probably not expected to live. I remember my mum telling me that a very large-busted lady came to see her just after the birth and asked my mother to pass her this little bag of bones. The lady held me snugly to her and it was said that the warmth of her bosom possibly saved my life. I've often thought about that: born in the middle of winter, two months premature and with very little medical help and, certainly, no incubators.

A couple of years ago, I spoke to Peter, my Godmother's son, and I asked whether he remembered me as a baby. 'Yes I do. A scrawny, tiny little thing that had to be dressed in doll's clothes because baby clothes were much too big. You were put in the doll's pram, as well.' One of my earliest memories is being in a pushchair and being aware of the feel and sound of the wheels going over the slabs in the pavement. I was probably about two.

We later moved to Bognor Regis, and I remember some funny things that happened in the 1950s when I was aged around seven. I was playing in the garden with my sister who was four. She asked me to go and get her a 'bloody orange.' She obviously meant a blood orange which we used to have quite often. I can see the horror on her face even now as she suddenly realised what she had said. We couldn't stop laughing for ages.

Around this time, I was at the bus station one day with my mum and the grown-ups were saying that someone had just died. I remember looking up into the sky, trying to see the recently-deceased 'rolling' up to heaven. I was very close to my Godmother, so it was a great shock when Mum told me she had also died. I remember clearly walking round with a heavy feeling in my chest and feeling lost. Mum was talking to my sister and me about it. I was crying and I asked them whether she would have taken her head with her to heaven. My sister, who always liked to be in charge, retorted: 'Of course she will have her head with her – she will have to see where she is going!'

I remember that around the same time as this, the grown-ups were talking in hushed voices about the storm of the previous night and that the shingle had come right over on to the main road along the sea front. Although I did not hear the storm, I sensed the seriousness of it. It was the storm of 31 January 1953 that wrecked the east coast and killed many people.

One other abiding memory that until quite recently left me with a fear of spiders was when Mum called me into the front room, saying we had a visitor and to come and say hello. I walked in expecting to meet a person, only to be greeted by the largest spider I had ever seen. It petrified me. It is only in the last five years that my fear of spiders has left me. I now look forward to the challenge of putting them outside!

DOWN ON THE FARM

by Sheila Darling

I was born on a farm in Chorleywood, Hertfordshire, in 1934, the youngest of six children. Our home was very much a farm of the time, with crops of corn, wheat and hay, all having to be harvested on an annual basis. One thing that strikes me about those days is that I am sure the weather was better.

We had about 50 cows needing to be milked twice a day; the milk and eggs from our chickens were delivered to the local people by my father and his brother, sometimes by van or by our horse and cart. We had 100 or more sheep and that kept us busy with lambs and yearly shearing.

I started school the year the war broke out. It was a small local village school about 30 miles from London. This meant we spent a lot of time in the local air raid shelters. Our school time was also reduced by half when the evacuees arrived in the neighbourhood so that they could spend the other half day in our places. Our family took in three girl evacuees; one stole money from the milk round, one was very home sick and the other, Sheila Michaels stayed with us for many years. In our village we had two butchers, one grocer, a post office and a small toy shop. On a recent visit, I noticed that the shops had all gone and our farm had been converted into apartments.

LIVING IN DICK TURPIN COUNTRY

by Margaret Dean

On a lovely autumnal day in September 1967, David and I were married at St Matthews Church, Stretford. My dad and I arrived in a beautiful big white car. I was carrying a Victorian posy of broken flowers because my dad had hugged me too tightly before we left home. I wore a white lace mini dress and my long dark hair in a lace snood. My granny nearly fainted. She was expecting a wreath and veil and a meringue. Not my style. For a minute, I thought she might demand we return the ironing board.

After the reception, my new husband and I set off for our week's honeymoon in St Anne's. We arrived in time to witness the turning off of the Blackpool lights and a week of the worst wet weather I had ever seen. No Seychelles or other exotic location for a 1960's honeymoon.

We had bought a tiny 350 year old weavers cottage at the bottom of a cobbled lane of similar cottages once known as Weavers Row. Unfortunately the name was changed to Livesey Street some time at the beginning of the 20th century, but to me it will always be Weavers Row. We did not have a single straight wall or floor anywhere, but we did have lots of lovely black oak beams. The big ones in the downstairs front rooms had holes in them that used to house the large hooks that supported the looms.

Weavers Row is in the village of Besses o' the Barn, supposedly named because the highwayman Dick Turpin had reputedly stabled his horse Bess at the inn there. A 15-minute walk towards Bury brought us to Whitefield, said to be named because the local home weavers had laid their cloth on the surrounding fields to bleach. The weather in those days must have been much better than we get now. Whitefield was where we both worked. My husband was an upholsterer, working for and learning from an elderly man who was considered locally to be an artist.

I worked in the accounts department at Halls toffee works where they manufactured the world famous 'Halls Mentholyptus Tablets.' It was a very uncomfortable place to work in the summer when the sugar attracted the wasps. With our beehive hair styles this could be scary. The consolation of the workplace was that if you ever had a cold, 10 minutes in the menthol room would help shift it.

Like most young couples in 1967, we had very little money. Almost all our savings had been used to pay the deposit on our cottage. The only new things were wedding presents and a bed from my in-laws and a 'Leisure Cooker with Eye Level Grill,' from mine. Everything else, including two carpet squares, was second hand, given in love by family and friends. We had a huge and terrible sideboard donated by David's Aunty Alice. Because she visited us at every opportunity, we had to keep it. My sister said it was a blessed relief when she died! With the sideboard gone, we were now able to accommodate a lounge suite. We had been saving up for what seemed like forever and I have never forgotten the excitement of going into the Co-op in Bury to buy it.

We had an outside toilet in the yard with a door that would not shut properly. You had to remember to keep the side of your foot against it. One day I was enthroned there and glanced up to see the local rag and bone man looking at me over the gate. I was mortified and my blushes lasted at least a week. This spurred us on to install our lovely new primrose bathroom suite. While making the space to accommodate this, we had to remove part of a wall and discovered an area of 'wattle and daub'. The local museum and newspaper photographed and reported this and thus we had our five minutes of fame. Over the following few years we worked hard adding a new kitchen, a damp course, new electrics and plumbing and so on. The fitting of new carpets was the best luxury for me. No more polishing lino or floorboards on my knees.

Our local school had an evening class on a Friday nights. It was called 'Homemaking.' I enrolled and learned how to cover a lampshade and how to make a pleated velour cushion cover along with many other 'necessary' items for our home. In the autumn, the course changed to 'Preparing for Christmas.' So off I went to learn how to make mincemeat and pies, Christmas cake and pudding and many other delectable treats. I thought that it would be nice to give my loved ones a homemade Christmas pudding to show off my new skills. I made them in basins and lovingly wrapped in red gingham tea towels. We had Christmas dinner with my family and when my mum tipped the pudding on to the plate it collapsed in a big flat dollop. We all laughed about it, but at least it tasted lovely. Everyone said the others I made were very tasty, but no one ever asked me for another one and I've never made one since!

How I loved my new life in that little cottage where we lived for nine years. Everyone who came to see us said it was a little palace - and I thought so too.

CONJURING THAT BULLDOG SPIRIT

by Sheila Dyas

The dogs of war of the Third Reich snapped and snarled their way across the frontiers of Poland and Czechoslovakia. Over the Welsh hills, ominous black clouds built up to send a clap of thunder rippling across the snowline as I hurried home from morning service that Sunday in early September. A storm was brewing. Entering the kitchen, my senses filled with the delicious roasting smells of Sunday lunch, the sound of a radio came from a room beyond. Father stood solemnly facing the window, listening intently as a voice like an icy dagger chilled the room. Mother, as if frozen to her chair, gazed into the fire in stunned silence, eyes unseeing. At the end of the news bulletin, Father took a deep, troubled breath and leaned over and flicked the radio off. Mother looked up: 'We're at war,' she said simply, striving to keep her voice steady.

The room grew quiet and nobody spoke for a while. 'I'll go and see how dinner is progressing,' she said at last in a return to her normal everyday voice (for the duration of the war, Mother wore a public mask of self-control).

Outside, small knots of worried neighbours began gathering in the streets. 'Who is this Hitler we've gone to war with?' a woman's voice called out. Yes, indeed, who was this Hitler who had suddenly turned our whole world upside down? A storm rampaged up and down the country that day – forked lightning danced across the skies. It was as though the Lord was filled with a terrible wrath at the stupidity of mankind and was voicing his disapproval. From that day on, a new chapter was about to open in all our lives.

Later, when daily reports heralded the outcome of a German onslaught, Father was sitting in his chair, reading the evening paper. 'Jerry dropped over 40 bombs on Frodsham last week,' he announced. Hitler was still trying to locate the oil refineries along the banks of the Mersey. During the few days up to Christmas, the Luftwaffe struck a fresh series of attacks on both sides of the river.

35

Among the casualties was Liverpool's St George's Hall, suffering severe fire damage. And the docks, of course, always the docks. Was this latest assault a prelude to something even more sinister? Hooton parish was swamped with scare-tales of gas attacks. 'Next time they come, they'll drop gas,' said one scaremonger. 'Gas to poison our food, gas to pollute our water, and gas to kill us.' Was there any substance to these rumours? Soon afterwards, when warning posters had appeared up and down the country, theatres and cinemas began refusing to admit anyone not in possession of a gas mask.

On one trip to the picture house, Mother and her close friend, Mrs Dulson, entered the dimly-lit foyer of the local King's Cinema. 'Have you got your gas masks?' the girl in the ticket kiosk asked them. Rather than go all the way home, the pair of them darted into a nearby shop, reappearing moments later carrying an empty box apiece hastily threaded with the customary piece of string as a carrying handle, therefore looking like the real thing. They didn't make that mistake again and, hurriedly purchasing two tickets, went through to their seats. Mother still remembered the time she had perched on a long, wooden bench in this same cinema. Every Saturday she and Aunt Violet would come in an open-top charabanc to the children's matinee. In those days, old Miss Peacock sat in the far corner plonking dramatically on a piano as she captured every mood of the *Perils of Pauline* and *The Clutching Hand*.

Lawrence Olivier smouldered moodily on the silver screen. His portrayal of Emily Bronte's *Wuthering Heights* anti-hero was melodrama at its best. My friend and I stared back in undisguised admiration. With the fury of a hurricane, the wind howled across the moors as the young girl stumbled aimlessly over the bleak terrain, the rain blinding her vision. 'Heathcliff, Heathcliff,' her plaintive cries were lost against the voice of the wind. The soundtrack seemed to increase in volume, expanding to deafening proportions. Suddenly, a superimposed message flashed across Heathcliff's face. 'There is an air-raid in progress. Patrons may leave, if they wish, but the film will continue.'

Mother and Mrs Dulson remained firmly seated, reaching out for the liquorice allsorts. No Herr Hitler was going to make them shift. Besides, what was going to happen to Heathcliff?

36

Two nights later, when it was Father's turn to see the film, a bomb, fell near St. Paul's church. The cinema shuddered alarmingly sending chunks of plaster raining down into the auditorium. For some reason, Father didn't wish to stay to see what became of Emily Bronte's tortured soul.

It was business as usual at the King's cinema the following Saturday. On the dot of 2 p.m. the doors opened to admit the usual rugby-scrum of schoolchildren. The billboards promised a star-studded programme of all the old favourites including the greatly anticipated weekly serial *Flash Gordon on the trip to Mars*. Changes were already taking place in and around the village. Berwick Road Primary School had been taken over by the Red Cross as early as 1938; the whole school being split up into separate units. One class was firmly entrenched in the scout hut along Heath Lane. Miss Baskerville and her infants had taken up residence at the Travellers' Rest. Three classes, including my own, were tightly packed into the Wesleyan chapel, leaving the top juniors to double-up with pupils at Father's old school - one mile away - in Childer Thornton. Our headmaster left to join the Royal Air Force, leaving his deputy to fill his shoes. This little Welshman spent the next six or so years tramping doggedly from pillar to post in all kinds of inclement weather. One cheeky pupil drew him a map. A second offered him the company of his pet poodle.

An army camp suddenly shot up in a neighbouring hamlet, the roads becoming congested with columns of army motor cyclists and convoys of trucks, filled with soldiers, going to ... hush. 'CARELESS TALK COSTS LIVES' warned the posters from every street hoarding. From our bedroom window, Elizabeth and I watched giant searchlights practising their search for enemy aircraft. Huge piles of sandbags were delivered to protect important buildings; on the roof of the police station, the siren perched like a large bird waiting for the first sign of danger to let out its banshee wail of warning. The village watched as low buildings with concrete roofs were hurriedly erected at intervals down every street. 'They're called air-raid shelters,' Father explained to us. 'If you're playing out when the siren sounds for goodness sake use them,' he stressed. It meant

Hitler's bombers were on their way. As it turned out, they were a potential death-trap and soon abandoned.

Now a heroic member of the Air Raid Precautions Volunteers, Father, kitted out in a navy blue uniform and tin helmet, cycled round the perimeter of the village on his regular tours of duty, protecting its citizens. 'Protecting us, my eyeball,' exclaimed Mother hotly, when unexpectedly she poked her head round the sand-bagged inner sanctum of the wardens' post and caught Father and Jack Webster asleep, each clutching an empty tin mug. A deck of cards lay strewn untidily across the floor; while in the background a battered radio crackled a 1920s number: *I'll See You In My Dreams.*

A strict blackout was soon enforced. Mother lined the downstairs windows with cheap black cotton cambric, and, to also save money, electric light bulbs were removed from their sockets in all the bedrooms. We undressed on the landing and went back to using candles. Anti-aircraft gun posts, manned by pockets of soldiers, mushroomed all along the banks of the Mersey; the coast festooned with barbed wire ringing off prohibited military areas. However, this did not deter our pet dog, Teddy McAllister and I stealing away to visit Eastham locks. Past rows of wooden huts daubed with green, black and brown paint. Past concrete barricades and 'No Trespassing' signs, where the soldiers always greeted us in a friendly manner, making a fuss of the little yellow dog. I suspected Teddy of coming here of his own accord - he knew his way round too well. Later in the war, when my Grandmother died, Teddy disappeared. Mother consoled me with the idea the soldiers had adopted him. But the little mongrel was never seen again.

From this vantage point of the locks, one could look down the full stretch of the Mersey where, left and right and strung out across the sky, huge, hydrogen-filled barrage balloons floated awkwardly, attached to the ground by steel wires. 'Even if the Germans do come, they won't be able to fly low enough to machine-gun us,' people said. What a fallacy that statement turned out to be. 'They won't come, you know,' my school chum, Billy Calladine, said matter-of-factly, as he fell in step beside me on our way to school 'Why not Billy?' 'Because me dad says they'll never get over the Pennines.'

Then came the mass exodus. Parents of children living in areas most likely to suffer bombing were urged to send them to the country where they would be reasonably safe. For three days, fleets of buses transported over a million children to stations in towns and cities where four thousand special trains took them to unknown destinations up and down the country. Several reluctant children from London arrived in the village. 'You'll be safe in Cheshire,' the authorities told them. But some were unhappy in their new surroundings and, not surprisingly, were constantly homesick.

TRAGEDY OF AN INFECTED NEEDLE

by Sheila Dyas

I was two and a half years old when my sister Joy was born. At six months, together with a baby boy the same age, she had the obligatory vaccination against smallpox. Both babies fell sick with septicaemia through the use of an infected needle. The little boy recovered, but Joy's condition worsened. It developed into pneumonia and just a month before her first birthday, my little sister died.

When my second sister, Rosalind arrived, I had just turned four. My mother and I were visiting my maternal grandparents for the day, when mum went into premature labour. Sometime during the early hours, I found myself looking down at a newly-born, quite ugly sibling. 'Where did this come from?' I wanted to know. 'Out of that bag,' the midwife informed me, pointing to her instrument bag on the floor. 'Don't be daft!' I answered rather rudely. 'It's too big to fit in there.' Just before breakfast, my father arrived on his bicycle. 'Is Amy here?' he gasped. 'She didn't come home last night.' My grandfather laid a hand on his shoulder, 'Come in, Frank, and meet your new daughter. Three important factors in these two short stories: In the case of the dirty needle; nothing was ever said or done, just swept under the carpet. GPs in those days were never questioned. Secondly, pneumonia was lethal. There were no antibiotics and penicillin had not been discovered. If it had, Joy would probably have had a long and full life. Thirdly, although a happy birth, there was no way of letting my Father know of the birth of Rosalind. Very few people had telephones. We moan and groan about the NHS and mobile phones, but can we do without them?

FLYING BOMBS AND ALL THAT

by Reg Easton

In February 1941, at the age of 12, I returned to my home in West London, having been evacuated with my school to Oxford on 2 September 1939. Travelling back by coach through the suburbs of London, I was amazed to see most shop fronts boarded up, with only a 12-inch window set in the middle.

The 'Blitz' was well under way in the early months of 1941, and the routine each evening was to wait for the air raid warning to sound. We then collected blankets, food, drink and a Davy miner's lamp to go into an Anderson shelter at the bottom of the garden. The Anderson shelter was made of corrugated steel sections bolted together to form a semi-circle, and covered with earth. It was named after the then Home Secretary, Sir John Anderson. I should add that sitting in a steel structure set in earth mid-winter was far from pleasant.

We lived hard by Wormwood Scrubs, a large public open space. The 'Scrubs' prison was also on the edge of the land. A battery of 3.7 inch anti-aircraft guns was sited on the area, together with searchlights. The camp was maintained by The Royal Artillery. When enemy aircraft appeared overhead, the gunners opened up, and searchlights lit the sky. The noise was tremendous. After several raids, I often cycled around the roads collecting shrapnel from the 'Ack-Ack' guns.

This was the normal existence for Londoners in 1941. The ensuing years of 1942 and 1943 were equally spattered with air raids. This continued until 1944. The Germans had by then perfected their V (Vengeance) weapons, and launched the V1 Flying Bomb soon after D-Day. On 28 August 1944, we were in 'the Anderson', our usual night time abode. It was approximately 2 a.m. A colossal explosion broke the silence. A flying bomb exploded three gardens away, smack on an Anderson. The family were killed outright. Our house was badly damaged while the smoke, dust and after-shock made us momentarily deaf.

In no time at all, emergency services, police, ambulance, first aid, fire and rescue were on the scene. The searchlight beams on Wormwood Scrubs were lowered to illuminate the area. The Salvation Army appeared in a van to dispense hot drinks and sandwiches. Equally, they gave us, the survivors, a cotton bag containing soap, flannel, comb, toothbrush and paste - all very welcome. Later we were evacuated to a local school, where the classrooms had been converted into bedrooms, complete with bed linen, washing facilities, and, of course, three-tier bunks. A week later we then moved to a requisitioned property in Chelsea. Our house was rebuilt some months later, and we reverted to it in 1945.

A MOST MEMORABLE STICKY BUN

by Hilda Eckersley

Before the war started and during Lent, the schools in Liverpool had a collection for the area's poor children, called *'The Good Shepherd Fund.'* All those who took part saved their pocket money to donate to it. I was lucky in that, each school day, I would wait at our front door to say goodbye to my Father and he used to give me a penny for sweets. During this Lent period, I gave up my sweet money to 'collect sheep' on a large chart on the classroom wall. After Easter, two or three children from each class were chosen to go to see the Archbishop at the Cathedral as a reward for our efforts. After Benediction, we handed him all the money we'd collected. Soon, it was my time to meet Archbishop Downey. He spent a few moments with each child. Then we were given a small bottle of milk and something in a paper bag.

When I opened the bag, inside was a sticky bun. My eyes lit up. It was the very best sticky bun you could imagine! In fact, it was so well received that I can't even remember meeting the Archbishop or even what he said. All I know is this sticky bun was the best thing of the day.

At Easter, 1937, I made my first Holy Communion. All the girls were dressed in white with veils and a wreath. Following this, it meant I could now go to Communion with the rest of the family. Afterwards, we had a party breakfast because we had not been allowed to have anything, even water, after midnight the night before. I remember the curate, Father Peter, a priest and monk from the Benedictine order, came in to see us and brought each of us an Easter egg. Me being 'Miss Know-All,' I told him: 'Sorry, father, I can't eat this during Lent.' Trying to keep a straight face, he replied: 'Oh, that's all right. I'll give you a special dispensation - so you can eat it today!'

When I was three years old we'd moved to a five-bedroomed house about five miles south of Liverpool city centre. I cannot remember anything before then. I was the seventh and last child in the family. I think previous owners of the house must have had a servant because all the rooms had bell pushes and the kitchen had a room indicator on the wall.

I started school at the age of four at St Austin's Catholic School, Grassendale, Liverpool. My mother took me the first day and after that Jim, my brother, aged 10, was given the job of taking me. He was a lad who whistled all the time and I was keen for him to teach me the art. My mother was not very pleased with the outcome, however. 'A whistling woman and a crowing hen would frighten the Devil out of his den,' she used to say. My maternal Grandfather, used to call and see us every week - and he whistled all the time. I also remember he smoked a little pipe with a silver top on it.

All my sisters were working and I would look forward to their pay day when they would bring me a little gift; a book or an apple, pear or banana, dipped in chocolate from the Lewis's department store in the city centre. I seem to remember that Lewis's had a small zoo on the roof or top floor of the building. I used to have my hair cut in this store, sitting on a wooden animal of some kind. After the haircut, I must have been told to sit very still because they singed the ends of my hair with a lighted taper.

In January 1938, my eldest sister died after a short illness. On the evening of her funeral, my father was smoking his pipe in the front garden and I went to join him to see what he was doing. He was looking up into the sky. It was lit up beautifully with bright lights. 'That's the *Aurora Borealis,* the Northern Lights,' he told me. It is very unusual to see them in this part of the world. In the November of the same year, dear Father died. He'd developed a growth in his throat and was only in bed for one week. That, of course, was a great shock for us all.

On the 3rd September, 1939, I remember coming home after Mass, sitting having breakfast and listening to the wireless when that famous announcement was made: 'War has been declared on Germany.' After the dreadful recent events, it was decided that I would not be evacuated, but that the family would stay at home together.

44

I remember the first the air raid sirens sounding one night. We all rushed downstairs, my mother pushed myself and Jim under the stairs and we ended up on top of paint tins and brushes and all sorts of tools. Needless to say, I was not very happy. But the next day, my brother put a mattress under the stairs and made up a bed. Later on when the bombing got bad, we used to go to bed there instead of upstairs.

At the start of the war, there didn't seem to be much bombing and so children who had been evacuated, started to return home. Parents who had houses large enough, started classes. We had about a dozen senior children and a teacher three times a week and I was expected to sit in with them and do my own work. They all liked to come to our house because my mother gave them orange drinks and biscuits. On the other two days of the week I went to another child's home for my own junior class and was also given homework to do.

One night, when the bombing had intensified, my eldest brother insisted we went up to the top of the road to the bomb shelter that had been built. So, in the pouring rain and in our dressing gowns and slippers, we trouped up the road. When we got inside the shelter, we couldn't understand why it was so light. Looking up we saw it had no roof! Even though the bombs were whistling down we couldn't stop laughing - so back home we went. Our Anderson shelter arrived when all the bombing had finished. I don't think we could have used it anyway as it was always full of water.

After the bombing eased off, the schools reopened again. But, of course, there was still the worrying threat and the sirens still went off. In this case, we would go down a path and past the graveyard to the church. The church's cellar had been made up into classrooms. Mind you, I don't think many lessons were carried out because some of the children were really upset – and so we just had some story reading.

In 1941, I passed the scholarship and went to the La Sagesse Convent. Later that year, I think the bombing eased off. But, from the age of 12 or 13, I suffered with migraine. The consultants I saw suggested cutting out the school homework, so I felt I was not able to keep up with the work and, consequently, I left school at the age of 16.

45

After a few months rest, I took the entrance exam to the Liverpool College of Commerce, passing that and starting a 12-month course. I then landed a post in the Almoner's Office at the Liverpool Radium Institute and I was there until I married in 1954.

THERE GOES ANOTHER DOODLEBUG

by John Edser

I was born in 1937 and lived in Stoneleigh, three miles north of Epsom, Surrey, until I got married in 1964. We had an 'unlucky for some' total of 13 houses in our road destroyed by bombs during the blitz. Our house had its windows blown in and the ceilings fell down, but we took our chances and stayed put. Until my father volunteered in 1942 and all the time I was at primary school, my mother said that when we left the house - Dad on the way to the City of London where he worked, or me to school - she never knew whether she would see either of us again. Obviously, it was a precarious time for all.

I remember me and the girl next door sitting on the step of our French window looking into the sky and watching as a VI Doodlebug went across the sky. If we could see it streaking past, we knew we were okay. But, if you heard it and couldn't see it, that was the worst and we'd scurry into our Morrison Shelter (the indoor one) - and wait for the bang. Nobody worried about the V2s - they were rocket bombs and went faster than the speed of sound.

Mum and I went on holiday to Teignmouth in 1944, packed like sardines in trains from Paddington. The passengers were beginning to relax as we got further away from London, but in the Maidenhead/Reading area, there was a large explosion in a field near to the track - a V1 saying goodbye to us!

I was a bit of an imp at the age of 10 or 11. I remember the winter of 1947-48, throwing snowballs at the hut of nearby building workers – always ensuring the men didn't catch us, of course. We also used to put a load of penny bangers down the pavement sewer traps and wait to see how many other stoppers would 'pop up' down the road. I was also a little industrious, too, and whenever there was a London 'smog,' I earned a few shillings by guiding cars, buses and lorries on my bike along the couple of miles of a nearby main road. I went to grammar school in Kingston-on-Thames, where I spent a very happy time - despite being told in our third year that the 16 years old age limit before taking 'O' levels had been dropped and we only had 1½ years before we actually took them. I went on to sixth form and it was there that I was introduced to medieval history and to Chaucer by two brilliant, if slightly eccentric, masters.

While in the sixth form, I got a holiday job that I kept until I left university. It was as a van boy for Lyons at their wholesale cakes depot based in Chessington, Surrey. We covered a huge area from Brixton Market to Basingstoke, and as far south as Forest Row in Sussex. The job taught me how to get on with people – something which certainly stood me in very good stead in my railway career and, I hope, to the present day.

I'd developed a passion for swimming and, at the swimming baths on school games day, we knew our session was followed by a group of young women trainee teachers from a nearby college. On our very last session before we left school at 18, one of our squad managed to get hold of some 'dry ice' and slipped it into the feeder bath from where the water was pumped into the main pool. We waited with bated breath to see the affect. We heard the trainees emerge and one, without any hesitation, jumped in followed by a colossal scream when she hit the freezing water. They called the attendant, who tested the water, found it much lower than it should have been - and hurried off to test the boiler!

I then went to the London School of Economics and met a world-wide cross-section of people. I studied Medieval History at LSE but also shared some joint sessions at Kings College, our rivals on the other side of the Aldwych. I have kept my interest in this right through my working life and, as people know, I am using it in some of my U3A presentations.

I had a long career in several senior capacities with British Rail. In 1963, I was transferred to HQ to work on the administration of Dr Beeching's rationalisation programme, the start of seven fascinating years at the centre of the major plans and reports of that era. Happily, it meant I no longer had to work unsocial hours and that left the way for the love of my life, Sally, and I to be married. We were lucky enough to be able to move to Chesham, Bucks, in mid-1965 under the GLC 'move out of London' scheme – a three bed semi came our way for £4,400.

In 1977 I was appointed to the post of Deputy Chief Controller of the London Midland Region at Crewe. This was a shift job (24/7) and with my colleagues I was responsible for train operations over approximately 60,000 square miles of the country. It was a fascinating period as besides all the normal railway problems, I had to deal with all aspects of human life. I had two babies born on trains between stations, managed to organise a bride to get to her wedding on time, got stranded honeymooners to their 'nest,' as well as a medical emergency – a kidney to be transported from Bristol to Lincoln on a summer Saturday afternoon.

NOT A BLADE OF GRASS IN SIGHT

by Richard Ellis

I was born at the end of the war and, like many others, we lived in a typical two-up two-down terraced house, tin bath and a toilet at the bottom of the yard. We had no garden to play in so we spent most of the time in the streets. We made carts out of wooden crates, made our own stilts, played glaggies (marbles), flicking cards, football or cricket depending on the season.

One of the things that sticks in my mind is that there wasn't a blade of grass to be seen; no trees and no flowers, either. The only green that could be seen came through the cracks in the cobblestones. I was about 10 years old when we moved to one of the new council estates that were springing up around Crewe. It was a whole new world; the house had three bedrooms with a bathroom and toilets upstairs and down, a garden back and front, encircled by privet hedges. The streets were clean and lined with new trees. We were delighted to have arrived in a place called Wistaston.

My brothers and I had found a new playground. Besides the Queens Park, there were fields and woods where we could build dens and climb trees. Brooks and streams were there to explore (and build a 'tarzy' rope to swing on). Yes, we had found a new world and we enjoyed it.

I left school in the winter of 1959. I didn't want to go where everyone else seemed to be going (Crewe Works or Rolls-Royce), so I decided to try for a job at Calmic (Crewe Hall). Now don't forget there was no industrial estate, just farms and fields. It was around Christmas time, a friend of mine said he would come with me and show me the way. We took what he said was a short cut across the fields. By the time we got there you can imagine what state I was in. I walked into the hall and up to the reception desk and asked if they had any vacancies. I think the receptionist took one look at me and decided there was no way I was going to work in the hall, so she asked if I would be interested in engineering. I was taken across to the engineering department and interviewed by the manager, Fred Archer.

After talking for a while, he rang my school and spoke to my form master. Putting down the phone, the conversation then went something like this:

'I believe you're quite good at football?
'Well I play for my school and Crewe schoolboys.
'Would you like a game on Saturday?
'Yes, I'll play for you on Saturday, but what about the job?
'Oh that's OK - you start on Monday.

So I started on the Monday as an apprentice sheet metal worker on £2.18s a week (I was earning more on my paper round!). The first day I thought I was in a foreign country. A lot of the lads came from the Potteries and I couldn't understand a word. For some reason, everyone had a nickname. There was The Sheriff, Badger, Carrot, Jinxy, Horace, Boris, Cedric and many more. I won't tell you what mine was. The one thing I will say is that I spent 16 very happy years there, working with a grand bunch of lads in a wonderful environment until the Welcome Foundation decided to get rid of the engineering department. Then, with engineering in my blood, I spent the last 25 years of my working life at...Rolls-Royce!

PUTTIN' ON THE FIFTIES STYLE

by Ann Farrington

My parents and I moved into Acton Road, Nottingham just a few months after I was born in 1945 and stayed there until 1960. But the time I can remember best was from the late 40s to the middle 50s. Our neighbours were all ages, although a lot of the children were fairly close in age. A Polish family lived on the other side of the road - the children all spoke English but the parents found it much harder to master the language. Next to the family was the district nurse – and she had a car! I cannot remember ever seeing her in anything else but her nurse's uniform. She had a similar build to Nurse Gladys in *Open All Hours*.

Our house was basically a two-up two-down. When you came in through the front there was a small hall leading to the living room and to the stairs. In the living room was a large fireplace with two small ovens at the side of it where newspaper and firewood were stored. The fire itself had a lever that was pulled down to heat the water and, on the lower oven, there was a small shelf at the front where I used to like sitting. The kitchen had large cupboards, a pantry and up on high, the electric and gas meters which you had to feed shillings into. Periodically the meters were emptied and a rebate of shillings was handed back. For clothes washing, Mum had an old copper before the Hoover washing machine made its appearance with its mangle/ringer on the top. Outside the back door was the toilet and next to that the coal house. I stopped doing handstands against the toilet door after I once came crashing through - it had not been closed properly. Upstairs were two bedrooms and the bathroom (minus the loo). The bedrooms were a reasonable size as they both could cope with double beds.

The house had a small garden at the front and a larger one at the rear where we played. Dad loved gardening and he grew soft fruit, tomatoes and flowers.

We had a radiogram which seemed a monster of a thing. Mum

and Dad used to play records like *The Nuns' Chorus, The Lost Chord,* songs by Mario Lanza and Gigli. I used to listen to *Uncle Mac* on Saturdays. Monday night was a firm favourite with Dad, he was always home to listen to *Journey into Space* with David Kossoff which frightened me!

The piano arrived when I was six and lessons followed - the practicing got harder when all my friends were out playing and I was perched inside. The church organist gave me my first music case. Mum bought the *Beano* for me and then later *School Friend* with the *Silent Three*. Enid Blyton's *Famous Five* series were some of my favourite books - particularly *Five Run Away Together*.

We acquired a telephone, a party line phone, which meant when you picked up the receiver and heard someone talking, it was the other party so the handset had to be replaced. If all was quiet you had to press a silver button to get the call signal and, hey presto, you could contact the outside world. In the early 1950s, our neighbours got a tiny black and white TV which had a large magnifying glass in front of it in order to see the picture. We eventually acquired, a 14-inch black & white RGD (without magnifying glass). Some of the programmes we watched were: *The Grove Family, The Appleyards, Mr Pastry, Billy Bunter, Dixon of Dock Green, Fabian* and *Quatermass* to name just a few.

There were no supermarkets in those days, of course, so most of the shopping was done at the corner shop. The grocery sold most things except fresh meat. Butter was cut off a huge block and wrapped in grease-proof paper; sugar was weighed out and put into blue bags. Cheese was cut with a wire. The best things were the jars of sweets. I loved Dolly Mixtures. In half of the premises was a dress shop selling good quality clothing for which you could pay weekly. Further away was the butcher's shop where, when you shopped there on a Saturday, you could leave an order for mid-week and he would pedal up on his bike with the meat in the basket (similar to Granville's bike in *Open All Hours*!). The Co-op milk float came up the road every day and the co-op baker's float three times a week. There was also a lady who came up the road with her horse and cart with a milk churn – she must have had her regular customers as well. Another vehicle came for a short time selling fruit and vegetables, it gave me the 'creeps' and fortunately did not last for long – it was a converted hearse.

All the children played out on the road. Games like 'farmer, farmer, may I cross your golden field', 'skipping under the moon and over the stars', hide and seek (annoying the neighbours as we'd hide in their gardens), jacks, snobs, whip and top, two ball, rounders, hopscotch, tick, piggy in the middle, marbles and conkers, knocking at doors and running away (enough said). We were never bored. One of the best places we went to was the coal yard and the saw mill further up the road. Once the place had closed (there were no gates) we were in there climbing over the piles of coal, hiding in the sawdust under the blade. The trouble was the owner lived opposite and many a night we had to run for our lives – dirty and dishevelled. I ended up in the copper being scrubbed by one angry mum on many occasions. When the snow arrived, we made fantastic slides on the steep hill end of the road - many a tired worker coming home would come to grief on it, much to our glee - oh what fun!

In 1957 it was a year of the 11-plus when my friends on Acton Road changed schools, some of us going to the same grammar school, others to private schools or the secondary modern, so the days of playing out in the evening were replaced by homework. The idyllic days of childhood fun and games started being replaced by 'pop' records (*Hound Dog, Rock around the Clock* and many more). Boyfriends started to appear on the horizon, along with *Six Five Special* on the TV.

The father of my friend was one of the first people in Acton Road to own a car, an Austin Seven. It sat proudly outside their house on the road (no garage), but I don't ever remember going in it. The seasons always seemed to be predictable (in my imagination or for real?). April brought the showers, summer really was summer, fog (very dense) and frost and snow for winter, then after Christmas the cycle started again.

I returned to Acton Road not too long ago. The street in my memory was much wider and longer. Everything had changed, but for me the time growing up there was one of innocence and a lovely childhood.

THE DAY RUDOLPH HESS DROPPED IN

by Christine Fleming

I was born in a sleepy village called Busby, just outside Glasgow, a month before D-Day in 1944, so I don't have any memories about the war except what I've been told by my parents. My father was in a reserved occupation during the war - he worked for a company called Barr & Strouds and he was an engineer working on instruments in submarine periscopes, a very delicate and precise job.

The most memorable happening in the village - and it proved remarkable indeed - was the capture of Rudolph Hess (Germany's Deputy Fuhrer and Hitler's right hand man) who parachuted into a field in the next-door village of Eaglesham on 10 June 1941. He was brought to our village hall where he was kept locked up and guarded by the 3rd Battalion Home Guard. Word soon got round that he wanted a meeting with the Duke of Hamilton to negotiate peace between Britain and Germany. Nobody seemed to know what happened to him afterwards, but the story was talked about long after the war ended. Of course, we now know he was tried at Nuremburg and sentenced to life imprisonment, spending the rest of his time in Spandau Prison, Berlin.

One of my first real memories was when we moved to Aldershot in Hampshire when I was three years old. My father had got a job in a Jeweller's shop as manager and watch repairer. He used to sit in the window and repair watches -I loved to go and see him and he'd make funny faces at me. We were also given a lovely old cottage to live in. It had a huge orchard, which I loved to play in with my friends.

Every summer we had many relatives visiting us from Scotland and we would all go up to London to see the sites. I remember feeding the pigeons in Trafalgar Square with my cousins and having photos taken with the birds on our heads. We also went to Scotland for holidays every year on return visits but the best part for me was the journey on the trains. Mum said I always disappeared and she'd always find me chatting away to various people and making friends. In those days, nobody thought anything about a child wandering around a train and talking to strangers!

One day, when I was six, my father told me I had to go and stay with my friend for the day and when he picked me up later he told me he had a big surprise for me. We got home and I was taken into my parents' bedroom and there in a cot was a baby. I'm afraid I wasn't impressed when told that he was my new baby brother Stewart - I thought the surprise would be a puppy. The next day a friend arrived with a puppy for me and a neighbour also brought me a kitten so I was very happy. I did accept my new brother after that and loved him to bits along with my puppy and kitten.

When I was nearly eight, we moved back to Busby and into a new council house on the former golf course - much to my dad's disgust. He had played golf on this course all through the war, and he revealed that we were now living on the eighth green!

I'd started at Busby Primary School, then at 11 moved to Eastwood Grammar School where I left at 16 with 5 'O' levels. I then went onto secretarial college to learn shorthand, typing and bookkeeping. It was the beginning of the Swinging Sixties so I had a great time except for the dreaded shorthand! In time, I got a job in a chartered accountants office in the middle of Glasgow. There didn't seem to be a shortage of jobs then, and if you fancied another I just had to go to an agency, which is what I did. They gave me a list of vacancies for shorthand typists and asked me where I would like to work. One job I really loved was in the offices of a clothing manufacturer in East Kilbride where I had to model clothes for the buyers. I could also pick a design and fabric and have a garment made up for me. What teenager in the 60s wouldn't love this type of job?

Glasgow was a great place to be at this time and I saw lots of pop stars live including Cliff Richard, Marty Wild, Gene Vincent and many more. I also saw Eddie Cochrane just before he got killed in 1960. I used to go to a club in a basement called The Cave - it was supposed to be like the Cavern in Liverpool. My dad didn't like me going there as he thought everyone was smoking and on drugs.

56

BENCHMARK BIRTHDAYS

by Enid Goode

I was 17 years and I couldn't wait for the year to pass so I could celebrate my 18th birthday in some style. I was sure it would be a grand occasion. Well, that first day of April 1951 ended up certainly different, but not in the way I envisaged. Unfortunately, I was struck down with a severe attack of pleurisy and I was sent to spend the next six months at Loggerheads Sanatorium in Shropshire. Arriving there the day before my birthday with my birthday cards in my suitcase, I spent my special day in bed, opening my cards and seeing numerous specialists.

While I initially viewed my 'isolation' with a degree of trepidation, I soon found the sanatorium an interesting place to be and I thoroughly enjoyed my stay there. As I did not have tuberculosis like many of the others, I was simply prescribed fresh air and rest. The sanatorium (or the 'san' as we called it), was on a massive site, surrounded by beautiful pine forests. Like others, I had to walk through the forests every day, at first for 20 minutes, then building up in stages to 1½ hours. It was so invigorating and I loved it. For an hour each day, I also had to have two sandbags on my chest to rest my lungs and make me breathe through my diaphragm.

Everyone was very friendly and we had lots of laughs. There were weekly film shows, men on one side, women on the other - unless you were married. We also had to work in the vegetable garden, picking peas and blackcurrants. There were patients of all ages and from all walks of life so there was a variety of interesting discussions. At one time, someone started Ouija board evenings which were eventually banned as they turned out very scary. I made some good friends there and I was sad to leave them when I eventually went home. So, despite my misgivings, I actually had a truly memorable 18th birthday.

The next milestone was my 21st birthday. I was working at Boots the Chemist and had just been offered promotion to senior-in-charge of the photographic department. As I knew little about photography and had only used a box Brownie or Kodak folding camera with black and white films, I was sent to the Rhyl store to be given four weeks tuition on the mysteries of photography. There, I learned about developing and printing and enlarging photographs, even tinting them. Guess when I got the call-up? Yes, just two days before I was 21.

Once again, I travelled with a suitcase-full of my birthday cards. My friend, Edna, also came along for a course in the fancy goods department. My birthday was on a Wednesday - at least it was half-day closing. I was determined to celebrate and rushed home to get dressed up in my best emerald green, gabardine suit, my black blouse, high heels and my black feathered hat. Edna and I went for a walk along the seafront until we came to the sandhills. We had a lovely time, climbing over the dunes and paddling in the sea, me in my pencil skirt with split up the side. Hardly the right attire! For my evening celebration, I suggested that we should be very daring and go to a bar for a Cherry B or a Babycham. But, Edna wasn't so keen, so we ended up celebrating with a frothy Horlicks in a milk bar.

Hooray, at least I was 21 at last! Was I now truly grown up and an adult? Perhaps not. I certainly remembered my 21st birthday, though.

My most memorable birthday of all, however, was on April 1, 2012, my 79th. My son took my husband, my Goddaughter and friend and myself to my daughter and son-in-law's house where I was toasted in champagne. Then, along with my handsome grandsons, aged 16 and 18, we went to a lovely canal-side pub for lunch and another toast. Afterwards, in the sunshine, with my loving family, we enjoyed a walk on Bickerton Hill. As we all sat admiring the beautiful views, I reflected on the day. What better than to be surrounded by my beloved family like this? I felt truly blessed.

BLACK (AND GOLDEN) MEMORIES

by Nancy E Griffiths (neé Black)

There I was lying wide awake and it was past midnight. Soon it was past one o'clock, then past two o'clock and still I was wide-eyed. To concentrate my mind, I started to think back over my life from the very beginning. I became so entertained by these pictures in the dark that I began to wonder if they would interest anyone else. As far as I can recall, my children have never said to me: 'Tell us about what happened when you were little, Mummy.' Were they not interested? I wonder why? So much has changed in the last 60 years that even an ordinary life like mine must have something they must wonder about, and amuse them.

I was born in February 1920 at 1, Lidderdale Road in Liverpool. My father had a furniture shop, on the corner of Lidderdale Road and the main road, Smithdown Road. There were two large glass windows with big gold lettering over which it said 'JOHN WATT BLACK,' and the door was across the angle at the corner. The furniture was arranged in each window leaving a diagonal path across the shop from the door to the corner where you entered the house, and the rear premises. I remember a high desk at the side of this door, on which stood a TELEPHONE! This was something special (well, I didn't think it special at the time, after all, I had always seen it there). But I was told – only a few years ago – that my friend thought it the height of sophistication, and was envious of the nonchalant way I used it (nonchalant at 6 years?). Nowadays, of course, everyone has a telephone, usually a neat lightweight one with lots of buttons to connect you to anyone, anywhere in the world. But not this telephone. No, this was a stand-up candlestick shape with a large ear piece which you unhooked from its arm, jiggled the arm up and down until a disembodied voice said – 'number please?' Then you didn't ask for a stream of digits, but: 'Operator please may I have Wavertree 14,' (or Central 56, or Royal something, or Sefton Park, or some other district). So much more interesting than all those

59

vague numbers - you could actually visualise the places you were calling.

Anyway, as I said, you entered the shop door, crossed the diagonal lino-covered path between the suites, and wardrobes, and chairs, and tables, said 'Hello' to Mr Leach (who looked after the shop) and climbed the two steps. Before me lay a dark passage leading to the rear premises where stock for the shop was stored. I didn't like that passage and would not go down it unless I had to, but by turning right I was in the house. In front of me was a carpeted passage to the front door. It was much lighter because over the front door was a large glass fanlight, with a back-to-front figure One on it in cream paint.

Had you come into the house the proper way through the front door, you would have climbed three spotless beige steps with a black shiny hand rail at the side. Spotless because they were cleaned with a 'donkey stone' each day by the 'Step girl' who was paid 2d for the job – and she provided her own bucket! The living room was off this passage, a lovely cosy room with a coal fire in a shiny black-leaded grate. It must have been quite a big room because I remember a square table and a sideboard as well as dining chairs and easy chairs, and there still seemed to be plenty of room to move. We had a canary on a stand in the corner – you never see canaries now, people have budgerigars. But our bright yellow canary sang so sweetly – I remember it died the same day as my grandmother (Grandma Rochell) and I always thought there was a connection. From the living room you went through to the back kitchen and another kitchen and out into the back yard. I can't remember much about the kitchens or the yard. I suppose I did play there but I can't even visualise it, yet I clearly remember my friend Dorothy Gore's yard – that had a strip of soil at the side with flowers and the back wall was whitewashed and there was a disgusting rabbit in a cage which fascinated me. Disgusting because it turned and sprayed you when you went to talk to it - and it got me every time. No wonder I remember it so well!

However, to return to my home, there was a steep flight of stairs by the living room door, leading to the sitting room and the parents' bedroom on the first floor. My goodness, up I used to go at a gallop because the stairs were dark. There was a turn half way and at the top in the angle of the wall was a huge mirror (put there no doubt to reflect a little light on the stairs). This meant you saw yourself as you came up and it made you terrified that you would see someone else as well. You see, I was a very timid child.

The sitting room was large, the same size as the shop. It had three windows overlooking the main road and one at the side where I loved to sit and watch the traffic going along Smithdown Road toward the Brook House. Traffic? Well it was busy for those days, but it would be horse-drawn vans and electric tramcars, with very few motor vehicles. There was a piano in the living room (how I suffered trying to learn to play it), a beautiful three piece suite, a China glass cabinet, and a gas fire that was always popping. This fire had a blue bowl filled with water in front, the idea being that as gas dried the air, the water kept it humid. But it always had matchsticks floating on it, flicked there by Daddy as he lit his everlasting cigarettes – much to Mummy's disgust! I still have the blue bowl, but it holds a plant in my lounge.

The bedroom next door to the sitting room had big heavy furniture with a huge wardrobe in which we used to hide. Well, that was until the day when Dorothy and I were inside and it tipped over. Luckily, it lodged on the end of the bed and we were able to crawl out. But that soon put an abrupt end to our game of hide and seek.

Well to continue our journey: up another flight of stairs to the bathroom at the turn at the top. This was an Arctic room not to be lingered in. Over the sitting room was another large room holding all sorts of treasures. I remember a billiard table where Daddy and various uncles played, a pianola, on which you sat and peddled madly to make the reels turn and play Home Sweet Home and other suchlike tunes. I can't imagine why we had the pianola, for the parents were not very musical, although I had been told Mummy once used to sing with the Philharmonic Choir (not that I inherited any musical ability!). My bedroom next door – grandly called the nursery – was up here at the top of the house. No wonder I was timid, I was miles away from everybody up there. There was a terrible picture on the wall of a stormy seascape, with big full moon shining on the waves, angry fierce waves. How I hated that picture. It frightened me so, but I don't suppose I ever mentioned it, for it was never removed. You just didn't question things like that, you just put up with them.

So that was my first home, so long ago, but still clear in memory, and I lived there until I was 10 – until it was all lost in the big Depression when life changed for us all. It was just different for me, but what a terrible change it must have been for Mummy and Daddy. From a big house and a busy life, to a small terraced house, gas lit, with a large old fashioned range in the living room and a copper boiler in the kitchen and no help in the house. There was also a new baby to cope with and having to live on charity. Still, more of that later. Let us return to the memories of living in Lidderdale Road. You recall that I mentioned Mr Leach ran the shop, well that was because of the other part of the business. Daddy had a removal business as well. We had two vans, huge pantechnicons, pulled by a huge cart horse. We had two vans and two horses, one looked after by Daddy and a little man whose name I forget, and the other looked after by 'Arthur' and a thin man. Arthur used to call me Miss Nancy and was great fun, and a bit of a tease. The vans and horses were stabled quite a distance from the shop and at the end of the day I was sometimes allowed to go with Daddy to settle them for the night. When we left the main road, I was allowed to ride the horses. I would only be about seven or eight and sitting up on those huge carthorses was a big treat, for I was high, high up above everyone else.

The only disadvantage was that I was riding bare back and I only had bare legs and cotton knickers. The horse had a hard bony spine which hurt. But I wasn't forgoing that ride no matter how painful it was! As the horse knew he was near his stable, at the end of a tiring and busy day, he would quicken his pace and little me would jiggle up and down on his back, clinging on for dear life. They were lovely beasts with big frilly feet and large brown eyes. On Sundays when the men were off, we had to go down to the stable with Daddy to feed and water them. I clearly remember one great black beast, a bad tempered old thing, who pulled away from Daddy's restraining hand when he was taken out to be watered, and chased Mummy and I round the yard until we took refuge in the small space between two vans. He stopped at the end and snorted and fixed us with his big black eye. I was always very careful after that to position myself ready for an easy getaway.

We had a little two-seater car, a Singer, that was kept in the yard during the day and we rode home in it after the horses were bedded down. It was great fun in that car, for it had a Dickey Seat at the back where I and any friends who came out with us used to sit. We went for trips to Formby and Freshfield, and the other way to the village of Hale and even across the Mersey at Runcorn on the Transporter Bridge.

Now the 'Transporter' was an experience to delight any child. It was rather like a ferry up in the air, rather than on the water. The vehicles and passengers drove on, the gate was shut, and the contraption was hauled across the water by chains until you drove off on the Runcorn side. I can't remember how many vehicles crossed at a time, probably depended on the sizes, but I should think six would be a top load. It was a long slow business, too, but it was well worth the wait because the only other way to cross the Mersey was on the ferry boat from Liverpool to Birkenhead, or to drive to Warrington and use the road bridge there.

The slow haul across the river was a thrill to me, as you could get out of the car and have a wonderful view. You could also see the railway bridge close up. There was a big shield on each end of the bridge; one on the Runcorn end, the coat of arms of Cheshire and the other with the coat of arms of Lancashire. The River Mersey was so busy in those days; liners, cargo ships, and ferry boats crossing to and fro. There were at least four ferry boats to different places carrying only passengers, as well as the luggage boats taking vehicles and animals. You could take a passenger ferry up river to Eastham, across to Woodside, down river to Seacombe, and then the longest trip of all to New Brighton, calling at Egremont on the way.

The New Brighton trip was the biggest thrill. I think it took about 45 minutes, and you had a wonderful view of the liners waiting in mid-stream or the cargo ships being pulled by tugs in and out of the docks as well as all the other comings and goings of life on the river. Whenever the cousins came over from Nottingham we always had to go on the ferry to New Brighton. Up on the top deck whilst the

63

parents sat, we could run round the deck playing tick and hide-and-seek. Now this was really quite a special time, for we were brought up very strictly and to be allowed to run around the deck of the boat was freedom indeed! When you disembarked at New Brighton there was another special treat. At the end of the pier beside the ramp, was a one-legged diver. 'Don't forget the diver,' people would shout and we would stand entranced to watch this poor man dive into the river. His friends or family would hold out shrimp nets on long handles for your pennies in appreciation. What a way to earn a living, I thought. I also wondered what they all did in the winter. We were full of admiration for him, however.

When you reached the top of the pier there were several exciting things to do – turn left and have a go on the paddle boats on the pool, or go straight up past the shops to stop beside the toffee shop. This had a window display actually making the toffee, big metal arms pulled and twisted the toffee into long gooey lengths, and the smell was delicious – sugar and vanilla – I can smell it still. You could also go to the tower and the fairground, or you could walk along the prom and go on the sand (it was clean in those days – even the water was clean enough to paddle in) or walk along to the lighthouse and the barracks on the shore, or even farther along to the Red Noses. These were granite rocks sticking out onto the shore, all ridged and coloured in layers, and looking just like a huge nose. So many things to fill the day, it was a wonderful treat.

I mentioned the cousins coming down from Nottingham. As well as their summer visits and trips across the water, they always came at Christmas and stayed at Grandma and Grandda Blacks' house, in Louden Grove, Princes Park. This was a big double-fronted house with a Laburnum tree by the gate (better known as Ladies Fingers) and lots of Lily of the Valley in front of the cellar windows. Several steps up to the front door, led into a wide hallway, with the dining room on the right and the drawing room on the left. The rooms were large, with heavy furniture, a big table in the centre, a large sideboard with a number of interesting ornaments including two silver epergnes with cut glass pickle jars (which always intrigued me). In the corner was the Polyphone. You put in your penny and it played tunes on the big steel discs you could see revolving inside. In the corner by the fireside sat Grandma Black. I cannot remember seeing her anywhere else (except visiting her in bed just before she died) nor did she 'do' anything - she just sat upright and stately and 'Queened it' over everyone. Grandda Black was a jolly friendly person, who enjoyed teasing us all. Still Christmas at 'Loudon' was wonderful. The Blacks and the Ecclestons all stayed in the house, whilst I stayed at home at Lidderdale although I was always anxious to go over to Loudon as early as possible to rejoin the others. Being an only child, I expect it was a great thrill to have someone of one's own family to play with.

Christmas dinner was a fine affair with about 19 or 20 of us sitting down, and Grandda carving the turkey, and Auntie Edie bustling about serving us all. Sometimes there was an overflow table in the bay window for the children, which was doubly enjoyable as it meant we were away from the grown-ups' eyes. The Christmas pudding came in flaming - more flames than I ever manage to get, and there would be loud applause. As Daddy and I would not eat Christmas pudding there would be a plain sponge for us and a lot of comment as to how foolish we were, not to like the star attraction. There were always two jugs of custard, one 'with' and one 'without' (the 'with' had brandy in, of course). The children had to have the 'without', though we still remember the time the jugs got mixed and we got the 'with.' They couldn't understand why we came back for more so soon!

After that enormous dinner I don't know how we had room for tea, but sure enough there would be jelly, and suchlike, with loads of cakes and mince pies, and we would all tuck in once again. After tea, the 'boys' (i.e. the uncles) would set to and remove the large dining table into the hall ready for the games and entertainment. The entertainment was provided by the children. Doreen would have written a play, and it would have been typed at uncle's office, and we were all given our parts to learn. Now I was in Liverpool, they were all in Nottingham, so the only rehearsal I had was during Christmas afternoon. We were banished to the top of the house where there was a big play room, and we had to prepare for the evening.

We must have driven our producer (Doreen) mad, because we were not very co-operative, but somehow we got it all together. I can't remember much about the plays except for one when we needed

65

the Ogre. Uncle Ernest was roped in to help, Cyril was put on his shoulders and the whole draped in a dressing gown. Cyril was terrified that he would fall off, so it was a very wobbly ogre who was more concerned with staying upright than with saying his lines. The 'stage' was the bay window of the dining room and we even had an unsteady curtain, which an uncle operated. It was always a great success, of course.

I remember when I was very small and attending dancing classes at the time, I did two solos. One was a repeat of a dance I had performed at the dancing class stage exhibition. I was a Charleston girl, all dressed up in pink lame; this was rather like a bathing costume in design, with bare legs and arms (but of course I had to wear a vest underneath) plus a big floppy beret that was very rough material and prickled terribly. Another time, I had been to the Empire theatre to see a ballet, and so performed the 'Dying Swan' as the ballerina Pavlova had done. Very moving. I didn't think I got the applause I deserved for this epic production! We were all expected to do something, as well as the play, and we all showed off of course. After the 'show' the games began, and the grown ups enjoyed this too, my mother was a giggler, especially after a glass of sherry, and there was always a great deal of laughter and egging on to make Elsie giggle.

Louden Grove was a lovely house, and so different, – when you went upstairs, first, there was a half landing and there was the bathroom with an enormous bath, and to get to the lavatory you stepped up a step, and there was a mahogany wooden surround to the toilet, a big one, not just a seat. There was one bedroom at that level; this was Uncle Neddy's room (Grandma's brother, who spent all his day beside the kitchen fire). Up again to the two front bedrooms where the grandparents slept and also Auntie Edie's room, and between the two rooms was a dressing room. This was actually used as a store room. It had big cupboards at the side and one thing kept there was a box of glacé cherries, for which I had a passion, and took every opportunity to pinch one. Up again was the boys room (Uncle Ben and Uncle George) and the big playroom, where there was a rocking horse, and an old standard lamp. This sticks in my memory because we always played Cowboys and Indians up there and I was always tied to the Standard Lamp – as the captured white girl. Later this part was taken by Jean and I was promoted!

I suppose that I was luckier than the other cousins as, living in Liverpool, I was able to go to Grandma's pretty well every Sunday. I think we had Sunday dinner at Louden and Sunday Tea at Ballington Street (this was where my mother's mother and father lived), then the following week it would be reversed. We walked from Louden to Ballington Street, and this was a very different sort of house. Much smaller, in a terrace of houses, and I always remember it being a very dark kitchen. It had a very big black range with a very small fire. In fact, that fire was a bone of contention between Grandma Rochell, Mummy, and the others. You see, Grandda Rochell was very mean with the coal. He always guarded each lump and was very sparing in the number of lumps he allowed to burn at any one time. Grandma Rochell was very kind and I always remember staying there when Daddy was so ill with Empyema, and she allowed me to help her scrub the kitchen floor. It was a red-tiled floor, and it was a great treat to clean it. (Well it was for me then, though I can't recall ever having considered scrubbing floors a treat since!). Another treat was to be given a twist of paper with a mix of cocoa and sugar. I suppose it was like chocolate, but anything that was different from what you got at home was special.

There was a piano in the front room, which I was told that Uncle Bert played, but we didn't see much of Uncle Bert, as he, and Uncle Fred were at sea by then. I cannot remember much more about Ballington Street. I suppose we must have met George (now living in Cardiff) there and his mother Auntie Jenny, and also Auntie Edie and her husband, another Fred, and Auntie Alice, but I don't remember seeing them there. I remember the lavatory was at the bottom of the yard, I remember the pavement outside the house was made up of small grey tiles and I recall listening to the Salvation Army band playing at the top of the road. Tired after our visit, I knew it was a long, long walk to the tram home. Ballington Street isn't there any longer. The area was rebuilt and I expect it's a lot more comfortable for the residents in the new modern houses than in the back-to-back terraces they replaced. I also recall about this time that Mummy and Daddy went out every Wednesday night, as the shop closed early, and I particularly remember being caught sitting on the front door step with the maid when they returned one evening. No doubt the maid was as nervous as I was in that big house!

I remember starting school at the Morrison – that was where I met Dorothy Gore, with who I am still friends – she lived a 10-minute walk away in Claremont Road, also off Smithdown Rd. We visited each other quite a lot, and I especially liked to be at her house for Halloween, for her grandmother used to toast sliced apples in front of the fire, which we ate piping hot and sprinkled with sugar. Then we used to duck for apples in a big bowl of water. Great fun. The year was always divided very firmly into various festivals. One didn't have Father Christmas appearing in October. October was the time for duck apple night, followed by Bonfire Night, then the exciting visit to the Grotto in December, and the Christmas holiday, taking the holly down on twelfth night and burning it in the fire, then my birthday in February, with a party for my school friends, and then came pancake Tuesday, Lent, and eventually Easter.

Easter was a quiet festival, everywhere was shut on Good Friday and we always had for dinner, fresh salmon, green peas, and new potatoes. Now in those days there were seasons for food as well as for everything else, and I can't imagine how we would manage to get green peas and new potatoes in April, but it is a firm memory in my mind. So on to the summer; I can't remember going away on holiday in those days, though we did go to Nottingham, when Auntie Bessie and Uncle Ernest lived in Clipstone Avenue and Doreen and I had a few high jinks when we got together, but those memories are later, when I was a bit older – no doubt all of 11 or 12! I used to travel alone to Nottingham, in the care of the train's guard, always on a Sunday because it was a cheaper five-shilling day return on a Sunday – Liverpool to Nottingham one week, and Nottingham to Liverpool the following week – so the holiday had to be arranged to fit in with these trips. Earlier than that I only remember going on Sunday jaunts in the Singer to the seaside somewhere. I suppose that was because the parents could not leave the shop for a longer period, or it just was not fashionable to go away on a summer holiday.

Eventually came the Big Depression in 1930 and Daddy became bankrupt and the shop was shut and we moved to 40 Gorsedale

68

Road. I think the removal business was kept on for a while, but finally even that went and life became very different. A new baby appeared on the scene in February 1931, too, and this must have been quite a shock to Mummy. After so many years, to happen in these circumstances when so short of money must have been terrible for her.

I started school at Arundel Avenue which was quite a long way away, but I had saved up and bought a bicycle - it cost £2.10s. and I bought it all myself. So I was able to cycle to school and home each mid-day for dinner. There was always a hot meal, and quite often squashed banana and 'top of the bottle' as cream for pudding! It must have been hard work for, by this time, Mummy, a trained dressmaker, was sewing to make extra money. With a new baby as well, I wonder now how she managed. Daddy did not qualify for any unemployment – or dole – as it was called, as he had been self employed, and he did all sorts of jobs. I remember he was working the markets at one time. I do not know what he was selling, but I know I was very ashamed at the idea. Proper little snob, I was. He also worked for Grandda Black still on the removals – Grandda Black had a furniture shop and removal business too – but, with Uncle George and Uncle Ben working there, I don't suppose there was much need of extra help from Daddy. I don't think we went short of much, although I did suffer having to wear Doreen's hand-me-downs, which I thought a bit infra-dig, but I was well aware of the difficulty money wise. I used to deliver the completed dresses Mummy had made and was delighted to be sometimes given a 6d tip from the ladies I visited.

Nothing much stands out about those years. I hated that house and the fact that it was gas lit. I was terrified to have to go up to bed carrying a lighted taper, and have to cross the dark bedroom to light the gas lamp. I used to talk all the way up, the conversation getting louder and louder the farther I went away from the living room. Dorothy Gore had left the Smithdown Rd area too by then. They went to live off Brodie Avenue in a modern house, which I envied greatly. We still visited each other often, although by then we went to different schools. Dorothy went to Aigburth Vale High. I had been put down to go there too, but it was not possible to pay for me by

69

that time, and as I failed the entrance scholarship, I had to go to the Central School. I remember that when I sat for the scholarship, I had a 'recall'. This was for the borderline cases who had not quite got sufficiently high marks. The reason I failed was strange really; I could not do decimal arithmetic, and there were decimal questions. The reason I could not do decimals was because when at the Morrison, I came next to top in class 3, so I jumped class 4 and went into class 5. Decimals, however, were taught in class 4, so I missed out and no-one bothered to explain them and it was all a complete mystery to me: a bit like the old proverb – 'all for a nail the battle was lost'. Still it was a good school at Arundel and I do not think I lost much.

It was a church school run by C of E nuns, although still under the Liverpool Education Authority. They were very particular, and we were well taught, especially in basic subjects, but also deportment and speech were considered important. We had eurythmics, and dancing, and I was in the Scottish Country Dance team and used to compete against other schools. Our sport was only netball as we did not have any sports grounds for hockey and the like, but I was a wow at netball! We had an 'apartment' on the top floor where we learned housecraft as well as cookery. I distinctly remember having to clean the bath and make a bed. I also remember making rice pudding in the cookery class and taking it home in my school case on the back of my bicycle. You can well imagine the mess it was in by the time I got home, but what upset me most was that I had been given a new pencil case for my birthday and the hot rice pudding really spoiled it. It had a zip top too, just at the time zips were new, and I was much envied. The end went all bubbly and soggy with the hot rice pudding! It broke my heart. I became Head Girl at that school in my last year, and I had a team of prefects, and we had all sorts of responsibilities. It was at the time of the Gresford Colliery disaster and I organised a collection to send to the fund, which greatly impressed Sister Vida, the headmistress (I seem to have been collecting for charities ever since!).

I was still there at the time of the opening of the Mersey Tunnel, 1934, by King George and Queen Mary. The schools put on a display and our school decided we should dress up as a flock of birds.

70

We assembled on the steps of Liverpool Museum in William Brown Street. I was a blackbird and I must have made a hit with one of the boys from St Edmunds because he kept sending me notes by one of the juniors. This was quite an embarrassment to me and tickled the juniors no end.

The nuns were very particular that we should all wear our school hats and one of the jobs of the prefects was to see that this was observed at all times. Whether on the bus or tram or walking to school we had to see they all wore the school velour in winter – or panama in the summer. Because I cycled to school, keeping it on was a trial. This used to amuse Gwilym, or Dick, or any of the boys who accompanied me. As I neared school, I always had to put my hat on – to be an example to the girls. I eventually gave in and agreed to Mummy's suggestion of a piece of elastic under my chin, like the little girls wore. At least it was easier than chasing my hat down the road.

We didn't take the School Certificate in my school so I went on to attend Skerry's College, which was in town. I used to travel by train from Mossley Hill station to Lime Street every day, and I think I went home for lunch also, though how I managed it seems a mystery as it was quite a walk at each end, but I certainly cannot remember having lunch in town. After an all girls school, it was quite a change to attend mixed classes, and the only thing which stands out now is that the boys organised a sweepstake on the Grand National. Betting was not anything I had come across before, and so it was all great excitement. The result was special, too, as I'd drawn the winner, Reynoldstown – so collected the large prize of 2/6d for my 6d investment.

We were attending Dovedale Road Baptist Church by now, this was a very go-ahead church and there was a big youth attendance. There was the G.A. (Girls Auxiliary) for the girls and the boys club met every Friday. There was also a scout group, a guild, a choir, and they all had social evenings, so there was always something going on. This is where I met friends that have stayed with me ever since. Church on Sunday night was a 'must' – all the girls sat along one row and all the boys together along another. If they could arrange to be on the row behind they were in their element, as they teased us at

71

every opportunity. We all gathered outside after the service and paired off for our evening walk. We must have been 16 or 17 or more by then, so I am jumping ahead too fast.

To return to the years between 1931 and 1937, they were not particularly eventful. Small things that were important to me still stick in my mind; Saturday supper of boiled onions with butter and thin Hovis bread, for instance. Mummy would be torn between the economy of cooking them on the fire in the range, which made the pan disgusting sooty black, or on the gas stove which was more expensive as they took a long time to cook. Sometimes we had spare ribs, which meant Mummy had to go all the way up to Penny Lane (whilst I looked after Victor) in order to get them at Woodson's. She used to leave it as late as possible on a Saturday afternoon as they were then cheaper. They were delicious too. These were simple pleasures really, but made special and exciting by the way it was always contrived to be a secret treat for when Daddy came home. Mind you there was one treat for Daddy which I could not stand and that was tripe, ugh, I simply couldn't face the stuff.

As Mummy was a dressmaker I was always quite fashionable, by adapting the clothes that were sent from Doreen, or making dresses out of quite cheap material. Of course we all wore gym slips to school, but even these had to be in fashion. We predated the mini skirt by 30 years, for the shorter your gymslip the smarter you were. I suppose it must have got out of hand because there came a decree that when you knelt down, the hem of the gymslip had to be so many inches from the floor. Mummy's greatest achievement whilst I was at school was my first long dress for the Seniors Party. It had a pale pink chiffon bodice to the hip and exact matching pink lace skirt, and cap sleeves. The neckline was draped with a chiffon roll of material held at one side with a diamanté brooch. It was truly beautiful and was quite a hit.

As Mummy was very busy dressmaking to help with the money we needed, I often went to Nottingham to Aunty Bessie's for my holiday. The most exciting was the visit in October, the school was closed for the week – it was called 'Teachers Rest' – and, as this was the time of the Goose Fair in Nottingham, I could not miss it. This was at first held in the Market Square, in front of the Council House, but later this was landscaped and had flower beds and sunken walks and was made very attractive and then named Council Square, so the Goose Fair was moved to the Forest. It was a magical time, we were taken at night when all the stalls were lit up, there were crowds of people and everyone was happy and jolly, and it was so exciting. I loved to buy brandy snaps - these were a Goose fair speciality and I never saw them anywhere else for years and years. You clutched them until they were sticky and chewy and absolutely delicious. As well as the usual attractions, there were things like stalls displaying the flea circus, or the fattest lady or inviting you to step in and box with the experts. There was lots of music and gaiety and noise of the traction engines, and that peculiar smell of oil, and wet grass, and people, and toffee, and candy floss – absolutely wonderful. As we often did not get home until 10 o'clock it was quite the highlight of the autumn for excitement.

Doreen and I always had a good time together, sometimes we were banished to sleep at the top of the house at Clipstone Avenue. We had midnight picnics, crouched on a sofa in the window, in the moonlight. The food had been saved during the day, a paper napkin can conceal the odd piece of sandwich or cake or biscuit slipped off your plate and sneaked up to be stored in the bedroom. There was an advantage in wearing knickers with elastic round the legs – it made a great hiding place for small parcels! We were aided and abetted by the maid who looked the other way many a time when we were 'helping' to clear away in the kitchen.

As Grandma and Grandda Black had died, we all met in Nottingham for Christmas at Auntie Bessie's, in Clipstone Avenue. We still continued with the children's entertainment, and one year, Victor who would be about 20 months, and I, did an acrobatic performance. We practiced for weeks beforehand. Victor must have had a wonderful sense of balance and no fear, for I would lie on the floor and hold him on my feet or knees and toss him around. He loved every minute of it. I bet that Mummy had her heart in her mouth – but it was a great act.

The most outstanding Christmas entertainment at Clipstone was the year that we, the children, suddenly decided that we were too old to act, so the 'grown-ups' said: 'All right, we'll show you, we'll do a pantomime.' Well, it was a riot. All the aunts took male parts, and vice versa. Uncle Ernest was Cinderella, Auntie Florrie was the Baron, and was dressed up in Uncle's plus-fours. Mummy was Prince Charming and was dressed in pyjamas, Wellington boots, and Doreen's school velour hat with a feather in it. Uncle Jim was the Fairy Godmother, draped in a lace curtain, and the Ugly Sisters were the Goodchild boys (friends of the Ecclestons, who must have been in their late teens or early twenties), and they were clad in Auntie Bessie's dresses and had orange peel teeth, which gave a lot of trouble and obscured most of the words. I can't remember who else was in it, but I know that Auntie Bessie was laughing so much that she set everyone else off. It was a tremendous show, and we were absolutely stunned at the sight of our 'sedate' parents acting the goat. No doubt we thought them too old to be so giddy, but they must have only been in the late thirties or early forties. They thoroughly enjoyed it even if we were overcome.

Another memorable time in those teenage years was one when I went with the Ecclestons on a summer holiday to Cornwall. En route, we stayed the night at Stratford-upon-Avon, and we went to the Shakespeare Theatre in the evening. One dressed up to go to the theatre, and although we did not wear evening dress, we certainly had our 'best' on. It was quite an event for me. I remember much more about the building than about the performance, which was *King Lear* (a bit beyond me) but the theatre I thought wonderful. We went on to Crantock, which is outside Newquay, and we stayed in a funny house in the village.

The trip to the shore was across a field and a range of sand dunes and on the first day I lost my purse there. It had all my holiday money, 30 shillings, and that was quite a good sum, and I was so upset. I was penniless, couldn't even buy a 'Snowfrute' (a triangular shaped ice lolly) and I was so aware of the shortage of money at home I would not write to ask for more. It was the hottest summer for years and everyone caught sunstroke or suffered in some way, except me, which was strange as I was so fair. We took trips in uncle's car to Lands End, which was much more remote and unspoiled and romantic than it is now, also to St. Ives, Falmouth, and Looe and Polperro. It was all lovely, and we had such fun, even the

74

DREADFUL Cornish pasties that our landlady dished up caused more merriment than disgust.

Another holiday from those years was one that I went on with the family and Doreen came too and we went to Cleveleys, outside Blackpool, and we stayed in a house where you had two bedrooms and a sitting room. This was a place where you bought the food and the landlady cooked it for you. It was quite a usual arrangement in those days. You had a sideboard in the room in which you kept your provisions. Every morning, you went to the shops to get the meat or whatever for that day and present it to the landlady, and it was presented to you at 1 o'clock for your dinner. It was quite an economical way of catering. I can still see that sitting room and the sideboard - maybe it has stuck in my mind because we broke a vase. I don't remember who did it, but I know we went all over the place to try to replace it. We could not, of course, and we were charged for the breakage. Mummy was very put out about the cost, as she thought it a tatty old thing anyway. There was a little funfair at Cleveleys, and there, it was the first time I heard the remark when one of the stallholders shouted to me: 'Come on dear, open your purse and let the moths fly out!'

In 1937, finances must have improved as we moved from Gorsedale Road to 44 Wayville Close. It was so exciting to go into a new house. Actually, number 44 was the show house, and although there were others ready, Mummy insisted that we wait to go into this one. Something about the plaster on the walls would be drier as the house had been in use, I recall. The deposit on that house was £65 – I suppose relatively it was just as hard to find as a deposit is nowadays. We liked this move as we had a garden and we had electric light again, and no wash copper in the kitchen, and no range in the living room. I can still see that house as clearly as when we were there: the green patterned carpet in the sitting room and the green suite with tassels on the arms of the chairs, the glass display cabinet with all the treasured china pieces - the Coalport that Mummy and Daddy had collected in balmier times. The living room with the square table in the bay window, and the brown leather couch and the wireless in the corner all come flooding into my mind: the kitchen with the NEW gas cooker, and the Acme mangle, my own bedroom, with the big double bed, and the very small bedroom which was Victor's.

I had started work by then, as a probationary teacher at the Everton Road Nursery School. I cycled every day, and had to be there by 8.30 a.m. and it must have been 8 or 10 miles away. How fit I must have been then, for the job was pretty strenuous at times and there was always the cycle ride home afterwards. I was paid the tremendous sum of five shillings a week, plus my meals, when I started work, and I gave Mummy 2/6d, and kept myself in extras quite easily. When I progressed to 7/6d a week, I managed to clothe myself too. Mind you, either Mummy or I made all my clothes, but I managed to buy the materials out of my wages. I remember a superb brown wool coat. I bought the material at Blacklers and it was 2/11d a yard, and the coat had a big flared skirt. I had a tricky little brown hat with two orange pom-poms at the front, and brown court shoes, and I can tell you I felt like the 'Bees Knees' when I went to Dovedale Church on Sundays.

We had a lot of innocent fun in our 17s, 18s and 19s with the crowd of young people at church, all our interests and parties and socials and play rehearsals, and the stream of different boyfriends. There was never a dull moment. Bank holidays were always fun, for we always made up a party to go walking to Chester or Caergwrle, or Loggerheads. We would meet at Central Station and catch the train to somewhere, walk and walk and return home tired out after a wonderful day in the open air. In the winter we often had Monopoly parties on Saturday nights - it was quite a craze, having only just come out, and was a great hit. We went mostly to the home of Joan Morris' (now Joan Honeyman and living in Canada) or to Dorothy Taylor's (now Dorothy Lee and living in Heswall). It was quite a long walk home after these Monopoly sessions, but we didn't have to worry about safety as young folk nowadays are worried. Why, I recall on my 17th birthday I went to the Rialto with Dorothy Gore to see Jessie Matthews in *Evergreen*, and when we came out it was snowing and we had to walk all the way home from town (the trams soon stopped if it snowed). This included a long quiet stretch past the university playing fields, but I was not worried about safety - more about my poor cold wet feet, for there were no such things as winter boots. In fact, I always seemed to suffer from cold feet. Every Saturday afternoon we used to go to watch the boys' football team and standing on wet grass was agony. I wonder if they ever appreciated how we suffered to support their football efforts. With cold feet, and straggly hair (as it always dropped in the damp air) it was a supreme sacrifice. We had to dash home to dry out, hair into curlers, soak in the bath, and pretty oneself up ready for the evening out at dance, or social, or date. Attending any of those functions meant a long walk to get there, too.

Dancing shoes in a special little case, hair tied up in a scarf to keep it in curl, and Wellington boots if it was snowing - no glamour at all until you arrived and stripped off the outer layers. No wonder I like to go everywhere by car now! Dances were great to look forward to, as you did not know who you may end up with. We often went as a party of girls together, and the boys went in a bunch, you would sit on opposite sides of the hall and eye them hopefully, waiting to be asked to dance. Of course, you had your favourites - Stan Hesketh had long legs and was great in the quickstep and polka, we always enjoyed those together. There was not a bar at any of the dances I remember, but it didn't seem to matter, there was plenty of excitement without alcohol.

We often had house parties during those teenage years, too, when you invited both boys and girls, and played various games. 'Wink' was popular, as you got a lot of kisses, 'Sardines,' 'Murder,' as well as guessing and quiz games, with loads of food, that you had spent all the afternoon preparing. Plus the joy of the walk home with 'someone'.

In 1938, there was a great deal of worry about the situation in Germany and the Munich Crisis made a big impression on us all. We were the generation who had heard all about the First World War from our parents, for we had been born just after it had ended. The horror of it was almost as clear to us as it had been to them, and we were frightened that it would begin again. Joan and I joined the ARP and learned about air raid precautions and mustard gas and phosgene gas and suchlike terrible things. Then, when the Munich Crisis did come, we had to help to issue gas masks. Folk who were unable to go the schools to collect their gas masks could have them fitted and have instructions on how to use them at home. I was entrusted with this job in my area. When I look back, I wonder how much confidence these old ladies, and young mothers with babies, had when they saw a young 18 yr old coming to tell them what to do in case of a gas attack. They were all so polite and so grateful that we had given up our Sunday to call with the gas mask and help them, but I wonder what they really felt. The whole population was scared stiff anyway and they probably felt glad they had not been forgotten.

We used to be very sarcastic to the boys about the fact we were doing something and they were not, till in the end they all went and joined the TA We were all so enthusiastic, so willing to do anything to help, so sure that war would not come. That is why, when in 1939 war did come, that all our crowd were immediately involved. The boys in their TA units were called up on that weekend of September 1, and I was soon on duty at the ARP HQ. The local ARP headquarters were in the Allerton Police Station and we girls were manning the telephones and getting instructions on the procedure of receiving air raid damage reports;   what to do with them, how to call out the ambulances and the heavy duty squads or the light duty squads to deal with damage.

I was on duty on the morning of the September 3rd when we heard that war had been declared. London had an immediate air raid warning and the whole country was frantically on alert. We were scared, but on our toes, forms and pencils at the ready, waiting to put into practice all we had learned. The 'All Clear' siren went soon afterwards and we all breathed again. In fact we didn't hear many alerts for a long time after that. We drilled and practiced and got ready for that dreadful time ahead when Liverpool had the terrible 'Blitz,' the period when we spent hours each night in the shelter in the garden or on duty at the HQ, and worked so hard. If I wasn't at work at what was by then called the "Civil Defence HQ" (which had moved to a big house in Allerton), I was helping at the YMCA canteen in town or helping at home. It was all an adventure and we took it in our stride, the fear, the worry, the work, the sleepless nights, the tackling of incendiary bombs, filling sandbags, making blackout curtains, and generally 'making do'.

As things got short and could not be replaced, it was a constant challenge to convert things. Nothing was wasted or thrown away if there was a chance it could be used for something else. Then came the food rationing; dried egg, very little meat, or eggs, or sugar, coupons for everything or queues when some special treat came into the shops and everyone dashed to get a share. The bread became coarse and lots of people came out in a rash because it did not agree with them. Mummy suffered quite a lot with this, erysipelas they called it, but eventually as we all got used to the bread, it cured itself.

I mentioned the air raid shelter. One had a choice of a huge square table inside the house, or you could dig a hole in the garden for the Anderson shelter. Most people preferred the one in the garden, as it seemed better than the idea of being buried under the house even if the table shelter was supposed to be strong. We had bunks inside, steps to go down, food in store, and we used to troop down when the siren sounded, taking blankets, and valuables and spend boring hours in the smelly dark. Someone always got fed up and would creep back to the house to make a cup of tea, and everyone else would be on tenterhooks in case anything happened to the brave one.

When these air raids went on night after night after night, you were apt to be so fed up that you stayed in bed and decided to take your chance. Mind you, the night we were bombed it happened before the siren went off. We were in bed and we heard the noise of the plane above, then heard the whistle as the stick came down. Next minute, there was a succession of explosions as four bombs exploded around us. We were so lucky; one fell in the university field, one between two houses, which made a mess of both, one in a garden and one on the letter box at the corner. My bed was by the window and when I heard the whistle I dived down the bedclothes in case of flying glass. Then I jumped up, opened my door and shouted to find out if everyone was all right. My voice sounded very odd, a bit croaky - so did the little weak answers. But we were all okay and soon, we pulled on our clothes and rushed out to help where we could.

Another night, we were in the shelter when a stick of incendiary bombs dropped all over the Close, and we rushed to put out the fires with the buckets of water and sand that everyone kept beside their door. What a shock we got when we tried to pick up the sand buckets. There had been so much rain that we couldn't lift them without help. I was terrified because we had just been informed at HQ that the new incendiaries were exploding ones, and the public had not been told about it. I tried to shout a warning, but no one could hear me for the noise. We dumped the buckets of sand on the burning bomb and ran away. I think one went off at the top of the road, and a young lad was hurt. But all the fires were doused in time before any damage in our Close.

Duty time at the HQ – which was called F 1 – could be boring in the extreme, with many hours of quiet, no air raids, then nights when it was too busy for comfort. There were a few hard beds and on a quiet night you could take turns in napping; this always made me feel very guilty, to be on duty, being paid, with nothing to do but sleep, when loads of folk were being worked hard, being bombed, being killed, and very frightened, and I was doing NOTHING. During the day we could take turns in the off-duty room playing table-tennis with the messenger boys, (I got quite good), or playing records and dancing. These messenger boys were schoolboys doing their bit, and we had a lot of fun with them, but I did not envy them when the raids were on as they had to go dashing off on their bicycles to deliver messages if the telephones had been put out of order and no contact could be made with the services we required to send to incidents.

Eventually by 1942, the Germans got sick of bombing Liverpool so very often, so it was decided that the staff of the centres should be reduced and the younger ones were no longer in a reserved occupation. We all started to look around for something else to join as we knew we would be called up and probably sent to a factory. We tried the Wrens, but they only wanted cooks and stewards by then, and that did not appeal to me at all. Then fate took a hand and I was called up. It was to be the ATS for me, and I had to resign from the Civil Defence ready for my call up. I had to go into Liverpool for a medical then wait for the papers to arrive. This meant I was unemployed - I was entitled to unemployment benefit – but the thought of going to the Dole Office horrified me. My prejudice against such a demeaning act was overcome by my need for money, however. I had been earning £3.10s a week – which was an extremely good wage for that time, as much as a man with a family would earn, and now there was nothing. So on to the tram I got and went to Garston to the Dole Office. Not only was it hard to go to the 'Dole', but to go to Garston, was the crowning indignity. Still I managed to put my pride in my pocket and go. I do not remember how much I got, but it was not very much.

I did not have to make many visits to collect it, as soon a brown envelope with OHMS arrived and I was informed that on August 22, 1942, I was to report to Harrogate to become a member of His Majesty's Forces. I was provided with a travel warrant for the train from Lime Street Station where we were met by an ATS corporal and a three-ton truck. Now it is not easy to climb into the back of a truck in a skirt, with no step or foothold of any kind. I was not very clever at this sort of thing, although some of the girls seemed to heave themselves in with very little difficulty, but I managed an inelegant scramble, and off we went to the 'barracks'. This was in actual fact the Queen Ethelburghers School, a very upmarket Girls Public school from which the pupils had been evacuated elsewhere, leaving all these scruffy ATS girls in their place. Our accommodation was in Nissen huts which had been put up in the grounds. We had double bunks and there seemed to be a great many girls in each room.

We started our army life with the usual medical followed by injections, which laid a lot very low indeed. I mean it knocked some girls out before the needle was jabbed in, the rest of us just suffered badly when the injection 'took' and we were quite poorly for a few days. We also had to be 'kitted out'. This meant parading in the Quartermasters store and having everything thrown at you - skirt, jacket, stockings, shoes, vests, knickers (passion killers – Khaki coloured celenese with elastic legs) toothbrush, comb, knife, fork & spoon and mug, and a kit bag to put it in, topped the lot.

We spent our days learning to be soldiers - drills, saluting, tests for this and that to see what we would be suitable for in our army life. There was also a most important visit to the tailor as our uniforms had to be made to fit, and we were not allowed out into the town until we looked respectable, and knew how to act and whom to salute. I can't remember much about the six weeks there. I know we

81

had various jankers to do and one time I had to polish the brass door knobs in the officers' mess, which I thought did not do much to help win the war!! We enjoyed Harrogate. There were some good canteens for soldiers there, and we soon learned that, wherever we went, the canteens attached to the Methodist churches were always the best. Warm, welcoming, with decent food, and usually a quiet room where you could get away from everyone for just a little while.

I was doubly fortunate in Harrogate for friends of Aunt Bessie, the Joblings, lived there and I always was sure of a welcome when I visited them. Toward the end of our initial training I was sent for as they wanted me to stay on and train as a drill corporal, but I did not fancy that at all, and said I preferred to go on to the transport camp. This turned out to be near Gresford in North Wales and so a little nearer home. The six weeks at Gresford was quite enjoyable. We went out every morning in vehicles of various sizes to learn to drive them. Several in the back, waiting their turn, one at the wheel with the instructor, and we trundled around the lanes on these 15 cwt trucks. The highlight of the morning was stopping for a break at some canteen or transport café, and the hope of a bacon butty.

It was a beautiful autumn, and the colours of the trees in the countryside around us were spectacular. Was it really so wonderful, or was it that I had never seen so much countryside at that time of the year? Whatever it was, I remember it vividly still. We spent hours and hours in a side street on the outskirts of Chester, reversing ambulances around the corner. Over and over again until that ambulance went round that kerb in a beautiful arc at the same distance from the edge all the way. I often think of that time when I watch the 'learners' at the bottom of Franklyn Avenue where I live, reversing the small car round the corner - what a hash they make of it, too. It wouldn't have pleased our sergeant at all. I won the competition for changing a wheel faster than anyone else – not that there was a prize, but I was very proud of that. It came to an end and we were passed out as competent drivers and I was selected to be a staff driver. I had seven days leave at home, then went up to Cartmel, as I was to be attached to the Royal Engineers.

To get to Cartmel in those days was a safari in itself, and I remember it took all day to get there, I arrived late at night, cold, hungry, and too late to get anything to eat, to be told I was not staying there anyway, that I was to go back to Carnforth. It was impossible to go then, so I was reluctantly given a bed for the night. In Carnforth I had to stay with a company of Ordnance ATS who were staying in a lovely old house called Warton Grange, outside Carnforth. These ROAC girls were working in Carnforth as checkers in a big storage depot, but I was to drive anyone connected with the RE Clerk of Works office. A lot of them were civilians and probably would have preferred to drive themselves, but they put up with me. It was an odd situation, for the girls I shared the barracks with didn't welcome me, as I was not one of the ROAC, and the men I drove didn't really want me there, and the army officer I drove was not around much - but I got around the countryside and there was a bit of fun as well. The officers at the depot had a very poor opinion of the ATS (no wonder when you saw the type they worked with); but I had a lot of fun with them and we spent a lot of time in the hotel on the corner.

We had to vacate the Warton Grange eventually, and we were to move to the Station Hotel. The day was set for the move, and a company of Pioneers were detailed to move the furniture. We went down with our kit bags and belongings to grab a room, to discover that the bunks had been dumped in the rooms but not assembled. Time went on and the men wouldn't hurry and it looked as if we would spend the night on the floor. At last I got a hammer from my vehicle and we put them up ourselves. I was to share with five clerks from the depot offices, four friends, and a corporal, and three bunks. As they were friends they elected to share two and two, and I had to share with the corp. What a madam she was too - all for claiming rank and grabbing the bottom bunk for the whole time, when the custom was that you shared; a week on top, and a week on the bottom. I sorted her out, however, corporal or no, I wasn't being done out of my share. Six in that room, three bunks, a wash basin in the corner, six lockers, book shelves each, it did not leave much room to spare, and one had to be very tidy, and the corporal wasn't - we didn't like her much, but I was fortunate as I didn't have to work with her.

I used to attend church as a Congregational - I tried them all, and this was the most friendly. I was invited into the home of a lady who kept house for her two brothers. It was a little terrace house in a side street. They were so kind, and asked me to tea on Sundays, or to just go and sit by their fire, and I spent a good bit of time there - so much more comfortable than perched on the bunk bed, top or bottom!

Eventually I was transferred to Quernmore Park, a vehicle-holding depot outside Lancaster. There were more people there, and we worked on servicing cars and lorries and then taking them in convoys to various parts of the country. Those convoys were an adventure in themselves. There were no signposts in those days, and although we had a route to follow, with towns in order of our journey, it was sometimes hard to find where we were going. We would return by train, always changing at Crewe - little did I know then that one day I would live there. We had transport provided from the camp to Lancaster or Morecombe, on a Saturday night, and always went to the pier to dance. The civilian girls did better than we did for partners, until a company of the Wessex Regiment came to Heysham. It brightened our lives considerably as they were a lot younger and more fun than the Pioneer regiments we often had to work with.

Mummy and Daddy had their Silver wedding while I was up there and I bought them some soup spoons from a jeweller's in Lancaster High Street. I often managed to get home at weekends as it was quite easy to hitch a lift south in a lorry. One was not as nervous of hitching in those days, the lorry drivers would do anything for you, and often went out of their way to assist you on your journey, or at least take you as near as possible to where you wanted to go. I always had a little money hidden away; now and then, Daddy would send me a ten shilling note to keep for emergencies, and it was kept safe in my pay book until needed, so I was able to afford the fare home, or part way home. I stayed at Quernmore Park until Daddy became ill and I was able to get a compassionate transfer nearer to home at Thornton Hough, Wirral. This was the estate of Lord Leverhulme which had been taken over by the army for a collection point for vehicles.

After Father's death I was allowed to live at home in Liverpool as long as I was able to get to the school to join the troop carrier to travel to Thornton Hough. This was quite easy as I had to drive the troop carrier so they couldn't go until I arrived. It was quite a business to get to New Ferry every morning as I lived a few miles out of Liverpool. I had to leave home about 6.30 to 7 a.m. to get a bus into town. As drivers, we of course wore trousers and boots, and the boots were like the men's boots only smaller and they had metal heels. So you can imagine the noise I made walking along those quiet suburban streets in the early hours - everyone knew I was on my way! The bus took me to James Street Station to catch the underground train and it was at the time the workers at Cammel Lairds shipyard were also going to work. There was little me squashed in the lifts amongst all these big chaps, and battling to get on the train. Actually they were very good and modified their language. When I alighted at Rock Ferry, I then had to catch a bus to New Ferry, walk to the school to pick up the transport and drive the others to Thornton Hough. All this was done in reverse at the end of the day. It sounds exhausting just to write about it, but then I was young and fit.

The vehicles that assembled at this depot had to be taken to various ports ready for shipment. These convoys could be quite dreadful – as I have said there were no signposts and even the names above post offices had been removed. Many times we would lean out of the cab window and call to a passer-by: 'Can you tell me where we are, please?' We always got to our destination, but I don't know how we managed it. One terrible convoy that I will never forget was a trip up to Glasgow to take some 15 cwt Canadian Fords. We always had trouble with Canadian Fords, always breaking down, and this time I had a very bad one. I had limped into Preston to the REME depot to be fixed up so the rest of the convoy had gone on ahead. We were to meet at Penrith where accommodation had been arranged for us. I trundled on through Kendal, all alone and started up Shap. Now I had heard about Shap and how steep it was but at that time had not driven up there. It was getting dark and I was a bit nervous but pressed on and then I BROKE DOWN – the electrics went so I didn't have any lights and I was soon in a bit of a state.

I managed to get to a transport café and went in for help. Eventually a kind driver of a 10-ton lorry said he would tow me to Penrith. After much hunting, the drivers there managed to find a rope, hitch me up and off we went. I had no ignition, no lights, it was dark and was I at the end of this rope like a conker on a string. Off we went very slowly for a few miles and then – the rope broke, and I was left floundering. My Good Samaritan realised that I was not with him and he came back for me. So we set off again up that steep incline and eventually reached Penrith. Too late to eat, and staying in a cold, cold house, in cold, cold beds. Once more the REME boys fixed up the truck and I crawled after the others, still going north through an increasingly snowy landscape, and again all alone. Crossing Douglas Moor with nothing to see for miles, across the fields I saw in front three Italian Prisoners of War. Well I was quite sure they were escaping and that they would hi-jack me and my truck so I put my foot down hard and that Ford went faster than ever before and I passed them pretty quickly. They didn't even look up – they were as miserable as I was and I supposed they were working on the local farms and on their way home, also cold and hungry. We got to Glasgow eventually, and sent the terrible trucks on their way to the poor lads overseas and we hoped they had more luck with them than we did.

We returned from these trips by train and, as we came south, I looked through the train window as we went over Shap to see the route I had taken in the dark. There was a nasty drop at the side of the road, and I was thankful that that lorry driver had helped me the way he did, or I might have been down there. (I went recently along the A6 and the road is now wider and well surfaced, and not nearly as steep as on my previous journey).

One of my last journeys was to take a vehicle to Manchester. Gwilym, my sweetheart, had returned from Prisoner of War camp and although we were forbidden to take passengers – he was in uniform and could, therefore, be picked up. He waited at the exit to the Mersey Tunnel and climbed in and we went to Manchester where we chose an engagement ring. I was demobbed in May 1946 and married in June. I then became a 'Griffiths' and so ends my 'Black Memories'.

DON'T TALK ABOUT THE WAR!

by Greta Guest

'Why is the sky red, Mummy, and what's that funny smell?' My mother quickly replied: 'That is London burning.' This scene took place in Hornchurch, Essex, in 1940. It was me asking the question, a small child looking in wonder, old enough to experience fear, but too young to fully understand what I was afraid of, and why. The full ramifications of war were strictly for grownups.

I lived on the edge of Hornchurch aerodrome in Essex during the Second World War. I knew about Spitfires. In the confines of the Anderson shelter I could hear them flying over. When the 'all clear' went, I was sometimes allowed to put my head out and watch them come back – I never counted how many and was never aware of how few, but felt very important calling out: 'Come on out everybody it's only Spitfires'.

The shelter was a dark, cold and gloomy place, the duck boards floated because it often flooded, and I laughed when things were floating in the water because we had to sit with our feet up. At home, I once heard a voice say: 'Why is this child in bed with her shoes on?' I knew why; I was afraid of getting left behind when they all ran for the shelters. After all, you see, I wanted to get to that dark gloomy place in double-quick time.

One night when we emerged from the shelter, our house had no windows in it. I heard someone call out: 'Doodlebug at the top of the road'. I knew about doodlebugs, you heard them drone, then go silent. Finally there would be a big explosion – somewhere. Soon after that, Mr Churchill broadcast that all children were to be taken out of London, but not the grownups. Grownups did not leave London during the Blitz, because it would have been seen as disloyal and not 'British'. Londoners looked down on people who did.

Evacuation was a big word. It meant new beginnings, new surroundings, new experiences, and strangers, but on the other hand, you could go to school, and not be holed up in the shelter so often -

and you could make new friends. What it did not prepare me for was discovering that people in the North talked 'funny'.

Now a scene change here: to Nantwich County Primary School. There were a few of us ushered into the school yard. I had my brother with me; the two of us part of the latest intake of evacuees. The resident pupils crowded round us: 'Say something, say something,' they chanted. So, in a broad London accent, I said: 'I'm as fresh as a daisy.' Well, how they laughed. But I thought they spoke funny, too. Didn't they realise it? The school bully was dispatched by a red-headed evacuee from Northallerton who had given me his coat to hold. I made a firm friend there.

Time passed and new contingents arrived from Guernsey. The whole of Ashford Grammar School, Liverpool, was evacuated to Nantwich Grammar, where my brother now went. Nantwich had its delights; the willows, waiting to see Toby the big horse who pulled the night soils cart and the dust cart. He was a town institution and much loved. Crowds of kids ran alongside him as he ploughed along the streets. We were like pavement sparrows with a freedom to roam, eating khali and liquorice, pop sweets that took the skin off your tongue. I heard, saw and ate things I had never before experienced. Home was different to London, too. We mainly ate rabbit, but I was told it was 'a bit of roast monkey', followed by rhubarb and custard. Any complaints were met with a bit of good old Nantwich: 'Get it down yer, there's a war on'.

And so there was. One night, Hitler came after the Beeston Oil Dumps. No shelters here - we crouched under the kitchen table with the plaster shaking down the walls. When Liverpool was 'getting it', we retreated to this 'safe place'. I had a special responsibility as well. As there was no bathroom or inside toilet, my job was to cut up the radio times into squares, thread it on string, and hang it behind the outside lavatory door. I took pride in my little job. There was the rug to help peg, as well, before we went out to play. There was an outside brown sink and a big barrel of rainwater in the cobbled yard. Our hair was always washed with water from the barrel. People were kind; I was allowed a kitten and, once, I learned to swear, listening to the men mending the telephone line up the pole. I put my head round the kitchen door and shouted 'bugger'. I didn't know it was a 'bad' word. I knew soon afterwards, though, because I got my legs slapped. I told the telephone men when they came down from the pole. How they laughed. They gave me some tea in a tin mug. I wished we'd had tin mugs at home - it seemed so grown up.

One day I was playing in the yard, watched by next door's Alsatian, when a man wearing a trilby hat came down the entry and into the yard. He held out his arms to me, but I didn't know who he was. My brother shouted: 'It's Daddy!' I threw myself at him, but I wasn't totally convinced because I had forgotten what Daddy looked like. My mother had visited us from time to time so I obviously knew her, but Daddy? It must have been a strange feeling for him when his own little girl did not know who he was. After a few days, however, I remembered him. My father returned to London and got bitten on the head by a rat in our shelter. It must have brought back the First World War experience as he once told me he'd seen rats 'as big as dogs'. He was in the artillery - I'd seen a picture of him in uniform.

Time passed and the scene changed again. Father was transferred from Fords at Dagenham to Rolls-Royce, Crewe, the house was sold to the RAF and, as both parents hailed from Warrington and Nantwich, the family settled here. The thing I remember is that I liked Nantwich and was happy here. The privations, compared to my home in London, meant nothing to me and, when I spoke, I now sounded the same as everyone else. The Cheshire Schools had done their work. Strangely, I remember that I NEVER CRIED during this time.

On reflection, how did the war change my life? Quite radically, I think. My life in suburban London before and during the blitz was mostly forgotten. Being taken to the capital to see the Queen, the days out to Whipsnade Zoo, our visits to Romford Market to see the puppies sold there, the elephant in the nearby park, holidays at Southend and Clacton, became distant memories. I am truly a Northerner now with just a vivid memory of the red sky over London burning. I believe in fate, and war meant I became a Northerner. Another turn of the wheel meant my two sons went to university 'down south', married southerners, and I now have six grandchildren – all southerners. Oh, I can tell you - they do speak funny!

CHILDHOOD RELECTIONS AND ROMANCE

by Gloria Horrocks

I was born in 1941 so remember little of the war. My father was serving abroad and Hitler had chased my mother out of both Sheffield and London, so I was born in Hampshire where my mother found a home for us all. I have a vague memory of the siren and something I thought was called the 'old clare' (all clear), and can still recall the rubbery smell of the gas mask, apple rings and the pale yellow powder in a blue packet that was dried egg. Other than that, the war passed me by although I still dislike the sound of planes at night which I think is probably a legacy of being hauled from my bed and taken to a shelter which I'm told did happen, even in the English countryside.

At about three years old, I contracted scarlet fever - then a notifiable disease - and was taken off to an isolation hospital. I remember little of this although I do recall I was in a room on my own and visitors had to peer at me through the glass wall at the end of the room - similar to being a zoo exhibit I suppose.

For my first four or so years I was the spoiled baby of the family until, one day, my mother disappeared then returned in a taxi carrying a bundle wrapped in a white shawl. Oddly, I can't place my father in this scene but, as this was the eighth such bundle, the novelty had probably worn off for him, or maybe he was still at work. Suddenly, the bundle was getting the attention that had, hitherto, come to me and the green eyed monster took over (although I did grow to love my baby brother in time). My mother told me years later that she had longed to see me when she had come home but I turned my back and refused to acknowledge her which broke her heart.

There is an early Christmas memory when, unable to sleep, I went downstairs to find my mother making a toy rabbit - I remember it was pale grey and had blue satin lining to the ears. Mother said she was making it for my cousin, David, but that she would ask Santa to bring me one like it. My rabbit duly arrived and, can you believe it, I was an adult before I realized there were never two of them. How dim is that? Christmas 1949 I received, amongst other things, a copy of *Alice in Wonderland* and *Through the Looking Glass* and a sleeping doll I named Claire Diane - I still have both and Alice remains one of my favourite books, guaranteed to make me laugh out loud. Claire Diane has lost some of her lashes and all of her clothes and her limbs are a little loose nowadays but she has been all around the world with me.

In 1946, my eldest sister married, I was five and was excited to be chosen as the only bridesmaid. I had a short, white, frilly dress (probably made by my mother who was an accomplished seamstress) white ankle socks but, sadly, not the white sandals I coveted - money being tight I had to have ordinary brown sandals which were suitable for wearing after the wedding. The night before the wedding, my mother tied my long, straight hair in rags so I would have Shirley Temple type ringlets, it was not to be as I ended up looking like a cross between Kevin Keegan and a shag pile rug. The church was opposite our house so no cars were needed as the reception was to be at home. Behind the church was a farmyard where we children were wont to play. I remember nothing of the ceremony but afterwards went out to play with my siblings and friends. We went into the farmyard to play hide and seek. I was 'it' and rapidly counted up to 100 (although I no doubt missed a few numerals) and ran out of the barn. In my haste, I tripped and fell, splat, straight into a large, fresh cowpat. I walked back into the reception liberally covered in cow dung and was rushed home. That, dear reader, is how to upstage your sister on her wedding day.

We had an odd religious upbringing, my father being Roman Catholic by birth but not inclination and my mother a Protestant who rarely went to Church but, nevertheless, said her prayers each and every night. As for we children, we went to church twice on most Sundays as well as Sunday school, my older siblings sang in the choir, rang the bells and pumped the organ, I had a go at the last two, bell ringing was fun but that organ took some muscle. At one point, we left the church and attended the local Methodist chapel which was much more fun as we had rousing songs like *I'm S-A-V-E D, I'm S-A-V-E-D* and *Build on the Rock*, with actions and clapping. I can't remember any of the sermons but the preacher, Oliver, was our coalman in his ordinary life.

My school days were not especially thrilling, I could read before I started school but mathematics were, and still are, largely beyond me. My love of literature, especially poetry, gave me the only speaking part in one Nativity play where I was the narrator, chosen because I was able to remember the whole of the relevant passages in the gospel - I think it was Mark – 'ye shall find the babe etc' - I can still do most of it when listening to *Nine Lessons and Carols* on Radio 4. In one play I was a shepherd and from sitting with my fellow shepherds in a circle, I had to rise to my feet, point and say 'Lo, a bright star in the sky'. Unfortunately, at the dress rehearsal I almost lost my part as my socks had fallen down under my long robe and I stooped to pull them up before uttering my single line - teacher was not best pleased and I got a telling off but was allowed to appear in the play.

I was severely bullied at primary school by an older girl who terrorized even the boys and was the leader of a gang; I was just one of her victims. After several months of bullying I told my brother in the hope that he would sort her out. Unfortunately, he being the gentlemanly sort would never fight a girl but one very cold Saturday, he and I walked past her house as she was in the garden with her sister. My brother called to her and she came out of the garden and slapped me hard in the face which really hurt, especially as my face was frozen. She was taller than me so I couldn't reach her, but something snapped and I totally lost my temper. Grabbing the front of her coat, red-faced and screaming, I shook her back and forth so hard the buttons flew off her coat and she retreated, crying. I had no further trouble from her and although we travelled on the same bus throughout our schooldays, we never again exchanged a single word. Indeed, she carefully avoided all contact with me. Her name was Benigna which just shows how misguided parents can be when naming their offspring. I'm not proud of my behaviour that day but it stopped her bullying me and may have also saved a few others from the misery I suffered. So far as senior school was concerned, I held the record for the most lost conduct marks in one term - its remarkable how one can lose something one never had in the first place. My crimes were very low level, running up or down the stairs, talking in class, passing notes and generally not paying attention. I did manage to get some 'O' levels although you wouldn't be surprised to learn they didn't include any maths subjects. After that I thankfully escaped the tedium of the classroom.

At 14, (Christmas 1955) my father bought me my first lipstick (dad actually thought I was too young but acquiesced to mum's suggestion). It was Yardley's Natural Rose No.2 to be worn only on very special occasions and certainly never to school, unlike children today. Living in a village had some advantages like access to other people's ponies - I was never to own my own horse - also the village dances where, accompanied by my mother, the adults taught me to dance (don't look at your feet!) old time and modern. The Gay Gordons was a favourite with the men as they could swing the girls and women off their feet. I liked the Veleta and the Quickstep. Rock and Roll had yet to be invented. My eldest sister could jitterbug wonderfully well – and you should have seen her rumba.

At 17, there was a first full on romance he was a friend of my friend's brother, he was just a boy with a motorbike and I didn't take much notice of him as I had a crush on another. One day, I received a love letter from the boy, I was surprised but oddly pleased and we spent the Summer together, fell in love, walked and talked, fell off his motorbike and kissed sweet kisses - anything below the neck was strictly forbidden, the permissive sixties still in the distant future. Summer that year was long, warm and perfect; we planned our life together and vowed to love each other forever but, our teenage dreams evaporated and, no, dear reader, I didn't marry him.

COUNTING (WET) SHEEP

by Jean Jackson

One of the biggest changes I have seen in the past 75 years has been that of annual family holidays. I suppose I was lucky because although we were quite poor financially (my Dad being a humble motor mechanic) we always had an annual family holiday. We used various forms of transport, ranging from an old 'banger' to a motor bike and sidecar.

The most memorable holiday I remember was going camping in Conwy (then Conway). This would be during the first years of the war. We travelled by motor bike and sidecar, with Mum riding pillion and us three little girls crammed into the sidecar, (don't ask where the luggage went I think we must have been sitting on it). It poured with rain nearly all week. We were staying in an old army bell tent which was like a wigwam with a central pole and there were camp beds like wheel spokes around it.

The rain started to leak in around the pole and, as there were coat hooks screwed into the pole with our clothes hanging on it, we soon found we had some rather damp items of clothing. My Mum begged Dad to call it a day and go home to Crewe, but he was adamant that we would still be able to have a good time and that the rain would soon stop (he was the eternal optimist - I take after him myself).

He did make one concession by going to see the farmer who owned the campsite and explaining that we were getting cold and wet in the tent. He offered us the use of an old shepherds' cottage which was literally one room with two beds and a small scullery with a stone sink at the back. It was a stone-built cottage so reasonably dry, but he had not told us that the sheep themselves were accustomed to pushing their way in for a nice warm shelter, so we were kept awake all night by the sheep butting at the door. We did have some adventurous games though rolling down the grassy slopes of Conway Mountain. When we did return home at the end of the week and related our experiences to friends and neighbours they were soon issuing the warning: 'If you want good holiday weather, find out when the Harrisons are going and don't go that week.'

The seaside towns we visited between 1938 and 1939 were either New Brighton or Rhyl. My sisters and I spent many happy hours playing on the beach and I particularly remember the New Brighton beach as there was this castle-like building which was called The Battery, and I used to think it was quite mysterious and romantic. We stayed in what was known as 'apartments'. This meant we had one large bed sitting room which contained two double beds, (my Mum and Dad in one and me and two little sisters all in a row in the other), a dining table and chairs and a sideboard in which we kept our dry food. Other food was handed to our landlady who kept it in what was called a 'meat safe' in her kitchen which was basically a small cupboard with a wire mesh door (to keep the food cool and the flies out). My mother would give the landlady instructions each day what to cook for breakfast, and then, if I remember rightly, we had sandwiches for our other meals, with perhaps fish and chips once or twice as a special treat

As I grew up and was engaged to my future husband we went by motorbike to Scarborough and stayed in a boarding house with close friends. When we arrived at our holiday home, we were soon shown to our rooms by the landlady; two girls in a room on the first floor, and the two lads in the attic. Things were very strict in those days.

The first time I ever stayed in a proper hotel was in 1950 when I got married and went to Llandudno for a week's honeymoon. The bill (which I still have) was £6.15s for bed, breakfast and evening meal for the two of us.

Times have changed so much over the years as tourism has flourished and, of course, is now big business all over the world. I have been lucky to get wonderful holidays over the years, ranging from family camping holidays with sophisticated frame tents and separate sleeping compartments, to a campervan when we were able to tour all around the UK - as well as memorable holidays in France. In retirement I have flown to very many exciting countries, including the USA, Cyprus, Malta, all of the Canary Isles, and Balearics. One of my favourites, Portugal, was the last foreign resort I visited with my partner before he died in 2008. Since then, like many older

95

people, I have enjoyed coach holidays to various resorts in the UK and hope to continue doing so - but what a range of contrasts from those early childhood memories.

FORTIES AND FIFTIES CORNUCOPIA

By Dave Jinkinson

What is my first memory? - I think it's the 1945 winter when I was nearly two. Perhaps my memory is from the photograph I found, but I'm pretty sure I recall building a snowman in the garden with my teenage girlfriend, Gwen, who lived three doors away. I recall that her dad, Mr Young, was the conductor for the Whit Sings when all the local churches and chapels paraded up our road and into the park opposite our house. I think he was a music teacher and I can remember they had a brass plaque at the front door - very grand.

My other very definite memory is going to the nursery which was also in the park - so an easy walk to school! I guess I would have been three years six months by then. I found it a bit boring, particularly when we had to lie down on camp beds for a rest after dinner. I never dropped asleep and I used to lie on my tummy and walk my fingers around under the bed until I was told off.

My first day at school is a clear memory. It would have been January 1948 when I went into the rising-five class, with Mrs Blinkhorn. I remember a large coke furnace in the corner of the classroom - no health and safety executive then though it did have a fireguard round it where our wet coats were hung after we got to school. One of my friends in the class was Mrs Blinkhorn's son, William, and I remember being very impressed that his mum was a teacher and very honoured to be able to go to my teacher's house to play with him. My other big school friend was Ian who lived round the corner from us. As in many families at the time, he lived in a shared house, with his mum, aunt and uncle (his dad was still posted overseas). The house was one of about six built around a yard which sloped down to a grate in the centre and with the 'toilet block' in the corner. Ian's dad was in the Far East during the war and had come back with an 'Anzac' bush hat which was in great demand when we played Cowboys and Indians. Early school friendships can last a long time and we are still friends today.

Talking of hats my dad had a tin one! Not from the forces, though, but as a Quaker. He was a conscientious objector during the war and was a stretcher bearer in the ambulance service, seeing the Sheffield blitz at its worst. From that background, my parents had many acquaintances from the Peace Pledge Union (PPU), and I remember them often having meetings in our front room. (Many years later, one of those same PPU members was the headmistress of the nursery school where my wife taught for some time). After the war, my parents also got involved with supporting German PoWs before they were repatriated, and I can remember two who came to our house, Dieter and Rudi. For some years after that we would get a small present from Rudi at Christmas, usually a carved decoration for the tree.

I remember one of my parents' friends (Uncle Jim to me) had a very glamorous image stemming from the war years. He spoke several languages and had apparently served in, whisper it ... military intelligence. His wife and daughter lived up the road from us, but Uncle Jim didn't. I guess this was the first time I had come across divorce - very rare back in the early Fifties, I think. He also had a very glamorous car - an Austin Metropolitan convertible - two-tone turquoise and cream with white-wall tyres - phew! (Princess Margaret also had one and so did Elvis Presley and Paul Newman). Another family friend, (Uncle Geoff, also divorced, had a Ford Pilot V8 and then a Ford Zephyr with a column change, front bench seats and, I really couldn't believe it, a radio. From that point I was hooked - steam trains, buses, trams? Forget them all! Cars became my passion, right until the present day.

I don't seem to have many memories of holidays. Certainly there were days at the seaside - probably on Sunday school outings. I can remember on one such outing, the whole of the party having to sprint up the beach, pulling my pushchair, as the incoming tide had caught them unawares and there a few pairs of wet shoes I think. Beach fashions? Well I found a picture of me wearing a rather fetching little number on the prom - a knitted swimsuit which I think was mildly embarrassing when wet.

Entertainment: chapel concerts of course and regular Gilbert and Sullivan performances come to mind, also tea and games at the

Friend's meeting house (I covered both bases - one foot in the local 'Congs' and one foot in the Friends). Whitsuntide was always a big event of course. On Whit Monday they had the Whit Sings in the park and the local kids would go over there early to watch the various church and chapel 'compounds' being roped off and the conductor's rostrum being built for Mr Young. Then it was back home for our best clothes and down to the chapel to line up behind the banner. The Whit parade came up our road so that was great fun to wave at neighbours as we walked past. At around five years old, I was even a page boy to the May Queen - what an honour to be able to hold her train and walk at the front of the assembled Meersbrook Congs!

After the war, my dad trained as a teacher of maths and physics. He was very impractical around the house but incredibly practical with early electronics. In the late Forties a fascinating shop, Bardwells - still going today - opened in Sheffield. This sold ex-army/government surplus hardware; ammunition boxes which were great for storing a young boy's 'treasures', old parachutes (I think my mum honed her sewing skills on parachute silk), maps of Europe printed on silk that would fold up and fit into my trouser pocket, and masses of early electronics from short wave radios to radar. Our attic was soon a storehouse for my dad's purchases and for his electronics magazines. One of my favourite pastimes was moving the various piles and boxes to make a circuit around which I could ride my tricycle when it was raining outside.

Soon, Dad's electronics skills progressed apace. While my Uncle Charlie could paper a ceiling in an afternoon and knock up an oak sideboard over a weekend, my dad made televisions! By 1953 we had one of the first 'tellies' in our road, just in time for the Coronation.

Since my early link to Mrs Blinkhorn, I think I must have had a fondness for teachers (and I did marry one). Through infant and junior school I was something of a goody-goody. Always in the top three in the Friday tables test; ink monitor supreme, security officer to take the dinner money to the school office, ensign for Mr Chandler, the headmaster, to take school notices between classes. In Juniors Four I was even chosen to ring the bell between lessons -

99

helped no-end by being one of the two boys in the class who had a watch (the other was Gunter Gregory - how on earth can I remember his name and see his face after nearly 60 years?). So, with the Coronation approaching, I asked Miss Prince, my Juniors Three teacher, if she would like to come to our house to watch the ceremony with us - and she accepted. All I can really remember from the day is a packed front room, a huge oil-filled magnifying glass in front of the nine-inch, government surplus, ex-radar television screen, ginger biscuits and coconut macaroons (my mum's specialities) - and that it rained.

I was so proud that Miss Prince had actually come to my house but when I told them all at school that Miss Prince had actually been to MY house and watched MY television - no one believed me. Well, as the song says: 'They all laughed at Christopher Columbus when he said the world was round'.

Televisions in the attic were only the start. By my teens and when ITV came on the scene, I was my Dad's apprentice as we installed new aerials and set-top boxes for his friends. Then astronomy came into the picture and our attic became the base for the local astronomical society to grind a twelve inch mirror for the reflector telescope they were building. By then, we possessed a car - a Ford Anglia - which needed a minor re-build most weekends.

Life in the Forties and Fifties was certainly never empty. Perhaps that explains why I still find it difficult to sit still for more than about an hour - unless it's in front of a computer.

Liverpool Blitz 1941

TV family 1960s

Tenement for demolition

Front Room 1957

Kitchen & toilet 1955

WW2 Anderson Bomb Shelter

Evacuees board train in Liverpool

Games on the bins

Primary School 1948

Traffic control in the fog

Holiday bus 1960

Mersey Ferry for New Brighton

Coronation TV 1953

A LOST WORLD

by Jenny Jinkinson

I was born in 1944, in Dewsbury, West Yorkshire, an industrial working class town. There were pockets of wealth; mill owners, professional people and business people, of course, but the majority of the local population was hard-working and hard-up too. Families tended to be large, women generally didn't work, and the men's wages were low. Our early childhoods were mostly devoid of men until they returned from the war. I always remember adults chatting and they always seemed to drop their voices a peg or two when discussing 'so and so up the road' - stories I was too young to fully understand.

I went to the local primary school where we had a rich curriculum which included much more than the 3Rs. For example: country dancing where boys and girls actually held hands together, maypole dancing each spring, sewing and knitting, singing, nature study, and we had a two week residential in the borough's country house when we were in 'the top class'. It was the highlight of every child's primary school life when we got the chance to live like those we only read about in books. There, we had dormitories to sleep in and fields to wander, streams to dam up and a shop nearby to spend our pennies. In the evening we played in the ballroom and each dorm created a 'play' to present to everyone at a performance on the last night.

I would have been eight at the time of the Queen's Coronation, and I remember making scrap books at home and school at this time and learning much about the Royal Family; the Orb, the Sceptre, the different coaches, Westminster Abbey, and the rituals around the whole event. We watched it at the home of family friends. I remember thinking it was far too long and drawn out and boring. It was a disappointment really to me after all the hype. I spent much of the time playing out and had to be brought in for the important bits. As a memento of the occasion, our borough council gave every child of school age, a blue glass mug with the borough's coat of arms on it, and chapel gave us a small hymn book. I've still got both items safely stored away (somewhere).

The family who had the television were friends from chapel. That was where we spent a lot of our leisure time. Chapel was, after family, the centre of our lives. We went twice on Sundays to services, but there were many events throughout the year such as bring and buy sales, concerts, parties to celebrate various things and personal events. There were pantomimes to produce, days out, not to mention special religious celebrations such as the chapel anniversary, christenings and weddings. There was an army of capable women who would turn up and make sandwiches, cups of tea and cakes for all while the children were allowed to play and explore in all the rooms. We had great fun and formed many good friendships as did the adults. My father's parents had been deaf and their social base was the Deaf Institute. We would go there as a family too, another exciting place to explore, and here, there was no limit to how much noise we could make!

In those days, children were allowed to play out for long periods, unaccompanied and unsupervised. Traffic was almost unknown, unless you count the rag and bone man and the milkman with their horses and carts. (I was asked to follow to collect what was left behind – good for the roses). We played across the street and in the park at the top of the street, enjoying freedoms not allowed today, to find our own way with not only games, but with decision making, rule-making, time-keeping and conforming to the group and so on. We weren't unruly in any way, but were well behaved and knew if we did do anything wrong, our parents would get to hear of it and then there'd be trouble.

The park was our playground in the school holidays. We made up wonderful adventure games using what was available and our imaginations, depending which area of the park we found ourselves in that day. Maybe it would be the field if the grass had just been cut, giving us unlimited dried grass to create houses with. Or maybe we'd be found making dens in the rhododendron bushes, playing at Germans v Us. At weekends, the park became a different place, a place where families walked and talked together and met with friends, visited the cafe or the park museum. Sunny Saturdays often saw a band playing in the bandstand and children roller-skating round and round on the smooth surface and sometimes, adults would be dancing on a summer evening. Sunday afternoon was definitely 'promenading time'; weather permitting, when we went in our Sunday best and walked around, stopping to chat to friends and neighbours. Children accompanied their parents and it felt good to be at their sides.

In many ways it was a trouble-free childhood. However I do remember there being things which were confusing. We went to chapel as I've said, and didn't mix with others who went to church, or more especially the Catholic Church. Similarly, those who went to the grammar school didn't mix with others who didn't, even if they'd been friends before. In fact fights broke out between Catholics and non-Catholics and between grammar-bugs and those who weren't. No-one ever explained why these things were as they were.

We had holidays in the summer, often a week at Scarborough in a B&B, which made us three sisters giddy with excitement, and it always lived up to expectations. As our Dad worked for British Rail, he'd have a number of free passes every year which enabled us to go away before we had our first family car. We also had regular days out to the country or coast with an aunt and uncle who had a car before we did - goodness knows how many of us piled into their car on the first expeditions, way too many.

As I got older, Saturday mornings would find me in town, in Woolworths, spending what little I had on sweets or maybe lipsticks. Older still, I'd be on the bus up to Leeds, the big city, to wander round the shops, trying on shoes in Saxone and Dolcis or clothes in C&A. I'd go with my girlfriends and we'd speak French and pretend to be someone we weren't. On a Friday evening, we'd go to church youth groups or maybe to the cinema - there were four in our town. Later still, we'd go dancing to the town hall, and even later, we'd go to Wakefield to the Mecca on a Sunday evening. It all sounds risky now, but we were safe. We knew what felt 'right' and what didn't. We were allowed to let our own judgment tell us if a situation or a person wasn't okay. We were on our way to becoming independent people - stepping out as young adults on our own.

103

HARD BUT HAPPY TIMES

by Sandra Kinnear

Mum and dad were married in November 1932. There were six children in our family although we all had very different early childhoods. My first recollection is picking gooseberries and putting them on a saucer Mum said I was two years old and we were visiting her two sisters and their husbands (they were brothers) in Sussex. I also remember sleeping on a camp bed and kicking a screen over on to my parent's bed. My uncles were both carpenters and one of them gave me a little wooden chair which I sat on all the way home on the train to Crewe, and kept for many years, Dad eventually turning it into a stool so that I could still use it.

My father was an exciting and innovative man. He idolised children and would do anything for them. He was always making things for us. Outside, we had a brick building divided into a toilet, coal shed and garden shed with their three doors next to one another in a row. Dad made swings so that us youngest three could use them. They had to be just the right height so that you didn't hit the toilet or the coal! We had a model railway running down to the bottom of the garden and one engine actually puffed out steam. Dad had a set of moulds to make lead soldiers. I can see the tin now – pinched at the top to form a lip – ledged on the coal fire to melt the lead. Then he would pour it into the mould and let it cool. We had hundreds of soldiers – some we painted. He made a large fort for my brother. He also made a large dolls house complete with lighting and furniture but, sadly, these got sold when money got tight.

He had a wood-turning lathe in the shed and I remember him turning whips and tops for every child in the street. We would colour the tops with chalk to form patterns when they spun. He also made yachts for us, complete with sails that we could hoist up. He had attached a sidecar to a tandem and we would pile into it to go to the paddle pond to sail them. But first we had to name them and so we'd stop at the railway station to make a nameplate. Here was one of those penny machines which stamped out the letters onto a metal strip and Dad would tack it onto the yacht. We hardly ever left the paddle pond with all three yachts as Dad would persuade one of us to give ours away to some boy looking longingly at ours (always promising to make us another one).

Dad could play the piano, banjo and accordion, too, and he only had to hear a tune to pick it up. The three youngest of us used to sit on top of the piano while he played and sang. However, the period between 4.30 – 5p.m. on a Saturday was sacred time for him and woe betide anyone who spoke while he took down the football results from the wireless and checked his coupon.

I always remember the time he showed me the secret way to open a small drawer in his shed. He had drilled a very tiny hole through the side of the cupboard and drawer and inserted a tiny headless nail. You just got a magnet to draw out the nail. I was truly amazed and still think it was an ingenious way to lock a drawer.

My mother was a very talented sewer. She could make anything and seemed to produce really lovely articles of clothing from cast off clothes and remnants of material. I remember having a white pleated skirt with red embroidered flowers on the straps. (Mum said, 'this skirt is special – nobody else in the whole world has one the same'). She once got me a baby doll for Christmas and knitted a gorgeous long dress, jacket, bonnet and shawl for it. She often came in early Christmas morning after a nightshift at the GPO sorting office to finish things off. We didn't get much at Christmas; maybe one toy and a sock with two shillings in the toe and an apple and orange and nuts. At one time, Mother made a beautiful bedspread out of blackout fabric. She stitched a large crinoline lady made out of brightly coloured bias binding on to it – something I cherished. She showed us how to make fancy dress outfits (mostly out of crepe paper) for our little shows that we put on in the garden. Also, vivid in my mind is a visit to Lovatt's fabric shop and choosing some white muslin material that had tiny embroidered coloured dots on it. Mum made me a party dress that was layers of tiered frills from the waist to hem. I adored it, more so because it was not made from any of my sister's old clothes. I was about five or six then.

I was almost six before I started school as my mother refused to send me to the school I was allocated. It was too far away. Other parents took their children on the back of bicycles but Mum couldn't ride a bike (nor did she have one). In any case the problem would have arisen again the following year when my brother started school. I eventually went to the Webb Orphanage until there was a place for me at West Street Infants. I then went to the newly built Totty's Hall School. Mr Challinor would walk between our desks with a cane in his hand, tapping his leg with it as we chanted our times tables, but I also remember him letting me use his Parker 51 pen. (It must have left an impression on me as that is what I asked for when I was 21).

Aged 11, I went to the grammar school for five years. Finding the money for the uniform was not easy but they managed somehow. I was quite good at sport and was in the school team for tennis and hockey (usually having to borrow a pair of hockey boots or tennis racquet). On the whole, I was happy there although there were one or two teachers I was afraid of. The geography teacher in particular – and I blame him for my giving up the subject even though I actually liked it!

On the whole I had a happy childhood. I loved my parents and I loved school. I enjoyed food and I wasn't a finicky eater like my youngest sister. Feeding us all could have been no easy task - I know a pound of mince lasted three days with more water, seasoning and dumplings being added each day. Every pay day, Dad would bring in a small bag of pear drops for us to share. Even the thought of them sets my mouth on edge now. I was not so happy about visits to the dentist or doctor. I remember the dentist putting this black mask over my face and I thought I was going to die. At the doctors, there were benches around the sides of the waiting room and you shuffled round to keep your place in the queue - sometimes waiting for hours.

We lived very near to open fields so had plenty of space for inventive games. We used to dig great holes and make 'dens' or 'hideouts'. There was a brook close by which we used to walk along jumping over it as we went and daring 'scaredies' to jump the wide parts. Someone always fell in and would come back to our house to wash out their socks before going home. The field on one side of the brook was very hilly so, in winter, we took our sledges and had a

106

great time (Dad made ours out of an old door). Again there were many casualties landing in the brook at the bottom. We would make 'winter warmers'. They were made from clay gathered from by the brook. You slapped it into the shape of a brick and cut a slice off the top to make a lid. Then you hollowed out the inside and put in hole into each of the short sides. Then it was filled with small sticks and rags and you lit it. You would put the lid on and run with it holding it up in the air. Air was taken in through the front hole and smoke came out of the back. It was supposed to get warm, but by the time we had finished making it and had run around with it trying to keep it alight, we were warm enough anyway.

We celebrated Bonfire Night on the back field with a huge bonfire, and mum showed us how to make treacle toffee to give to everyone. We would take a potato each to roast in the fire. We had our Coronation party there, after a procession around the streets dressed in fancy dress. I was a Hawaiian girl and mum made me a 'grass' skirt out of raffia and a lei garland with tissue paper flowers. My sister was an attendant to the Queen, dressed in a pretty dress, and my brother walked behind carrying the Crown on a green velvet cushion wearing a matching velvet cape with high collar!

One of my favourite games was marbles. We had marble mania in our street. We were lucky because we had grass verges and we would dig a small hole and aim our marbles at it. Our road was as smooth as glass and perfect for roller-skating. We had great races on skates and would skate until our legs were numb. I remember saving up towards some rubber-wheeled skates with ball-bearings which were a big improvement from the metal wheeled ones I'd had one Christmas.

Without doubt, most of my time was spent with dolls. I loved them and had several (all cheap ones from the market and different sizes). My mother taught me to sew, knit and crochet and every doll had a large number of outfits including underwear, swimwear, party clothes, nightwear, etc. I can't understand girls today who buy everything for a particular doll – it takes away all the fun – after all when you have dressed and undressed the doll, what is there left to do? I had one three inches high and even that one had a full set of clothes which I kept in a drawstring bag I had made. I remember taking a small Rosebud doll to Paignton on holiday and I was distraught when I discovered I'd left it behind in a cupboard in the caravan. Mum wrote to the camp about it and, fortunately, the people there returned it to me and I still have it today. Another memory of that time is that we girls would go around asking mums if they would let us take their babies for walks in the pram. Most of them did, which is hard to imagine nowadays. Groups of us would be walking around the estate pushing prams and pushchairs with real babies inside!

Then, there were the usual games like hide and seek and skipping. I remember our skipping verse: 'Jelly on a plate, jelly on a plate, wibble wobble, wibble wobble, jelly on a plate; paper on the floor, paper on the floor, pick it up, pick it up, paper on the floor; sausage in the pan, sausage in the pan, turn it over, turn it over, sausage in the pan.'

Also, we had a craze for two-balls against a wall. You threw the balls alternately against a wall, reciting a verse and making different movements to each line: *PK penny a packet, first you chew it then you crack it, then you stick it to your jacket, PK penny a packet*. I remember seeing a game of Monopoly in the newsagents and asked the owner if they would keep it for me if I paid so much each week until we had covered the cost. I took in half of my 2/6d pocket money and that of my younger brother and sister every Monday until we had covered its cost of 25/- (£1.25) and could then collect the game – a lot different from children nowadays.

I used to love going to church, chapel or Sunday school. We didn't go as a family – I would go on my own or with friends. I often went for the wrong reasons. I went to Ramsbottom Street Chapel so that I could be in the Christmas show where I was a Moon fairy and a Welsh girl. My friend went to Minshull New Road Chapel so I tagged along, and I also attended the congregational church on Hightown because I wanted to go to their youth club. In my teens, I settled on St Michael's and went to the church regularly and the youth club straight after the service – from hymn singing to rock an' roll. I even undertook a religious education course through Radio Luxembourg so I must have got something from it.

When we could afford it, we would go to the Odeon on a Saturday morning. I loved the films but, oh dear, the noise was horrendous. You could become a steward (keeping the children in line before going in) and then you got in free.

My mother insisted that we all help around the house. Each of us was allocated a job or jobs to be done before Sunday. I think we all dreaded being old enough to do the 'bathroom, stairs and hall'. The bathroom alone was a big enough job with eight of us using it. The stairs had to be brushed with a small, stiff hand brush and the hall floor was red tiled and had to be swept, washed and polished.

There was always a mass of washing (and ironing) to do, and I remember mum eventually hiring a washing machine with an electric mangle and which was delivered every Monday. Mum used to have some really good ideas. I remember her decorating our bedroom. She then took two drawers from an old battered set and turned them onto their sides. She papered the back (which was really the bottom of the drawer) with matching wallpaper and then fixed a glass shelf across each one. My youngest sister and I had one each to keep all our trinkets and treasures on.

Food was rationed during and, for a while after, WWII. We all had to take a turn at shopping which was at the local Co-op across the field - or the long way round over the cinder track. From aged 10 onwards it was nearly always me because I had a bike and could put the heavy bags onto the handlebars and push it home. Was I glad when the Co-op started a mobile shop (a converted single-decker bus) to our estate. Mum wrote her list in a little red book each week and the assistant would bring the groceries right to the door. Brilliant! There was also a farmer who still delivered milk from a churn on a horse-drawn cart. There was a period when both Mum and Dad worked and we were able to have a week's holiday. By then Dad worked in the railway sheds so he got free passes and we would go to Devon and stay in a caravan in early or late season because it was cheaper then. Prior to that, our parents would ride their tandem to Chester for a day out with us three in the sidecar.

The things I disliked most about my childhood (after my dad died) were mainly caused by shortage of money. I always seemed to be making cardboard cut outs for inside my shoes when the soles wore through; we never seemed to have a shilling for the meter; my brother's joke: 'Glad you dropped in Bob, I was just going out',

109

never applied as our meter always ran out!) Also, I felt ashamed at having to tell the rent man we would pay double next week (which Mum always did but I felt the stigma of it). However, both of my parents gave us their time, a conscience, an understanding of the need to care and share, and a sense of freedom that many better off children did not have.

I met the boy, whom I was later to marry, at Crewe Carnival when I was only 13. I had an instant crush on him and wanted no one else. We started courting seriously when I was about 16 and I got engaged to him at 18. He was a year older than me. He was a good football player and I would go and watch his matches. We married on 25th June 1966, and we have two boys. Both were keen footballers and a Lads and Dads football team was formed, which we fully supported. They took part in the Scout Gang Shows for which I made several hundred costumes!

We are now both retired. (David finished work through ill health).Our children are grown up and have children of their own. I'd like to think we gave them the same values my parents gave to me. The most precious thing we gave (and still give) is our time and, of course, our love.

BOMBS AND BALLOONS

by Margaret Lunt

I was born in 1934. During the war, a barrage balloon was bedded in a field across from the Rising Sun pub in Wistaston, just down the road from our house. It was through the park gates which were then an entrance to Rookery Hall. With great excitement and anticipation, my older sister and I would run outside every morning to see if it was inflated. Although this indicated an impending air raid, for two little girls the sight of it inflated and floating in the air gave us great delight and it is a happy memory that has stayed with me over the years.

As children, we were protected from the awfulness of war and we felt no fear or anxiety. The only inconvenience that I remember it brought was an air raid shelter being built at my school. It took up valuable space from the school garden where once a week we had gardening time. I wasn't very happy as this was the highlight of my week and the start of a lifetime hobby. Even when a bomb fell one night in the field across the road (the impact of which blew our windows out) we took it in our stride. The next morning we were all packed off to Grandad's house in Willaston while it was sorted. It was something different for us and we viewed it all as an adventure, just like the times we sat under the stairs or under the dining table whenever the air raid sirens went off.

I now realise how lucky I was to be living in the Cheshire countryside during this time - unlike the children from the cities. I remember seeing the skies flashing over Liverpool from searchlights, but fortunately my wartime memories were happy ones. Like seeing the barrage balloon or when my sister and I took great pleasure when the milkman would give us a lift on the back of his cart so that we could cross the fields to Wistaston School. During harvest time we would play hide and seek in the corn stocks in these fields. Sometimes we would be late home because we would stop and watch the threshing machine: - those were happy days!

111

SIRENS AND SHELTERS

by Barbara Maskell

I was born before the war and I was at primary school when it actually started. We used to have air raid practices when we had to get in pairs and walk in line down to the playground and the underground air raid shelter. There were a few forms to sit on down there and we probably had a sing-song or a story read to us. This was just for a short time, pretending there was a raid on, although I don't really recall one happening during the daytime. When the raids and bombing actually started, people put shelters up in their gardens or a joint one they could share with families.

We had a cellar and Dad decided to reinforce it with strong posts like pit props and he put all our beds down there so that, come night time, my brother and I slept there. If the siren did sound we were probably asleep and we didn't hear it. We were lucky as I could imagine that some of the shelters in the big cities must have been very uncomfortable to be in for any length of time. How much sleep they got and then had to go to work next day, I don't know. The thought of going to sleep in the cellar now horrifies me, but, as children, it didn't appear to bother us.

We were issued with gas masks because of the worry that gas would be used like in the First World War, but it never happened We were supposed to have our gas masks with us at all times. The boys soon realised that the checks and gas mask practices were on the same day each week, so on the other days they used to stuff their gas mask boxes with paper so they would be lighter to carry. I'm sure their parents didn't realise the tricks they got up to.

We had a barrage balloon near us on the Catholic Bank as it was called then, in St. Mary's Street, Hightown, Crewe. Now there is a block of flats built on the land, but we used to go and look at the large barrage balloon stationed there.

My uncle and family lived in Coventry. I do remember going there to visit them just before the war started. Coventry suffered very heavy bombing, of course, and had a great deal of damage done to it. Although their house was not directly hit, the windows were all blown out. There was glass everywhere; the beds, sofa, chairs and furniture. The house was eventually declared unsafe to live in and they were sent to Crewe, from where they had originally come. They had to live in one of the prefabs there which had been quickly put up to house families just like them and my uncle got a job at Rolls-Royce.

THOSE DAILY HEALTHY DOSES

by Brian McNair

My first schooldays were in 1940 when the war had just started. Anderson shelters had been built in the school gardens but they were never needed, we just had practice drills wearing our gas masks which we carried to school every day. The German bombers came over during the night, very rarely in daylight, although one did attack the Rolls Royce factory on Sunday afternoon early in the war. My Dad worked on a farm, so didn't have to go to war. I remember him coming home on his bike with a can full of fresh milk on his handlebar every night He also kept hens and grew vegetables, so all we didn't see until after the war were oranges and bananas. We had fruit trees in the garden - apples, pears, damsons, plums - so we didn't go short. Like most other children, I had to have my spoonful of cod liver oil and malt every day. I didn't think much of that, but in hindsight those daily doses must have helped keep me healthy.

We lived in an old house, privy at the bottom of the garden, sash windows which rattled when windy, and sometimes wedged with newspaper or small rubber wedges All cooking was done on an old Excelsior grate which had to be black leaded from time to time and this also heated the house. Sometimes, usually on a Sunday, a fire would be lit in the front room or parlour. A primus stove was sometimes used for the frying pan and the kettle which whistled when boiling. In the winter, a paraffin Valor stove was used to heat the bedrooms and hot water bottles were in regular use. We had no electricity until the 1950s and there was no gas supply in our village, so paraffin lamps were hung from the ceilings and we used candles in the bedrooms.

Wartime saw the windows with sticky tape criss-crossed on the glass and thick blinds to stop any light filtering out. One bomb did drop about half a mile away and shook the house, but no glass was broken. When the air raid warning siren sounded, I was taken by my parents over the street to my uncle's house. He had a cellar where we

114

sheltered until the 'all clear' was sounded. A brick air raid shelter had been built in the street, but we never used it. From the top of our street you could look over towards Liverpool some 30 miles distant and see the sky all lit up by the bombs being dropped there. It was said that the few bombs which were dropped in our area were by bombers jettisoning them while making their way back home after not being given the chance to drop them on Liverpool.

Schooldays went quite well, although until the late 1940s there was not much provision for sport. We had to play football in the school yard with old tennis balls. It was probably 1948 before the school had a leather case ball with a rubber bladder blown up with a bicycle pump, and then tied up with a lace. It hurt your forehead if you caught the lace when heading it. I remember I escaped having the cane while at school (which was always given by the headmaster), but did have the pump by another teacher. You were made to touch your toes, and then soundly whacked on your 'rear end' by his rather large PE pump. One lad who refused to bend over had the class in uproar because he said he had a big hole in his trousers. I don't think anyone wore underpants in those days. I know I was 21 and doing my National Service before I wore them!

FINDING AN UNEXPLODED BOMB

by Neil Parker

I was attending Church Street School, Wallasey, when the war broke out, and the government decided that all children should be moved from potential target areas to somewhere safer. One morning soon after, we all assembled at our schools with a few possessions and our gas mask in its cardboard box plus a luggage label tied to our lapel, with name and address printed on. We marched down to Seacombe Ferry Station about two miles away. The mothers were not allowed to walk with the children, but had to walk on the pavement. When we reached the station we all marched onto the platform, but the mothers were locked out, till after we were all on the train.

You can imagine the panic as about 500 frantic mothers ran up and down the platform, looking for their child to wave goodbye. My mother found me reading a comic and quite unconcerned, and had to bang on the window to attract my attention! One thing that has stuck in my memory is that on the platform was a Nestle chocolate dispensing machine. Like all little boys, if there is a button to press or a handle to pull, it's compulsory to do it. So I pulled it, and hey presto - out popped a small bar of chocolate. Fantastic, because it had never happened before and I got a chocolate bar for free.

When we arrived at Irby, only 17 miles outside Wallasey, we were assembled in the local cricket pavilion. We were given a brown paper carry bag with a few tins of processed food and a little fruit. Then the local ladies came in and, like at a slave market, they looked us up and down then said: 'I'll have that one or this one'. After a little while there were just two of us left, and soon the other boy was picked. I must have been the runt of the litter and if you can imagine being in a large wooden building and the only one left, it was lonely. I was taken by a lady to what seemed a big house, and introduced to her husband and daughter. I liked them but, from the start, not the lady.

My first meal with them was in the kitchen, and I remember her saying: 'Shush I can hear a funny noise.' We all listened. She said it had stopped so we went on eating. 'Shush, it's there again,' she said. It transpired she was referring to me making a noise when I ate. Although my mother and brother were staying in the village in lodging, where my father had sent them for safety, the lady, (I can only call her that because I don't remember her name), would not let my mother see me - she said until the end of the war. She even offered to adopt me, (no wonder Mum was crying when I did see her and, after a few days, Father had me back home).

It was May 1941 before the Germans bombed Wallasey. By that time we were on our second street shelter as the first one leaked rain so badly it had to be pulled down. My father had built bunks under the stairs in our three-up three-down terraced house. There was just room for my brother and myself. Mother sat just outside and Dad had to stand in the back kitchen, and he would walk up and down outside on the lookout for incendiary bombs. He looked like Stan Laurel because he wore his old bowler hat stuffed with rags, hopefully to give him some protection from shrapnel from our own Ack-Ack guns as opposed to the German bombs. We used to go in the shelter most nights, but only when the radio, tuned in to Birmingham, went off the air. The radio silence meant that, within 10 minutes, the bombers would be over Merseyside.

One night after a lull, Dad said I could go outside with him for some air. After only a short time outside he told me to look up and we saw what he thought were five parachutists: 'They must be from a plane that's been shot down,' he said. A few seconds later, however, he soon changed his mind: 'Crikey, they're aerial bombs,' he screamed. He almost threw me into the shelter when they went off. The blast blew him on top of me knocking all the wind out of me and the next morning we found that three roads had gone completely and part of my school as well. The bombing carried on for a few weeks more but most of it was centred on Liverpool.

One morning my Dad was due to go to work on his bike, but had only gone a few seconds when he came back and said it was still dark outside. It turned out that a barrage balloon had been shot down and was draped all over our roof and windows blocking out the light!

I had an interesting morning watching the airmen climbing all over our house getting their balloon back.

I used to collect shrapnel which was everywhere in the streets. But the best and biggest was found on the shore after the tide had gone out. One Sunday - it had to be a Sunday because my dad was at home and that was the only day he did not work - I had been walking along the beach for some time when I saw the fins of a bomb sticking out of the sand. I dug it out, and ran all the way home with it. I could hardly wait to show my Dad. I remember shouting 'Dad, Dad, look what I've found.' He took one look, snatched it off me and disappeared through the back door. He was gone some time. When he got back he just said: 'If you find anything like that again, don't touch it'. I never saw my bomb again, and it was only a little bomb, and would have fitted so easily under my bed!

During the bombing, the water supply to our part of Wallasey was cut off. The nearest water was a stand pipe near Egremont ferry, luckily at the top of the hill because it was very steep. I had a trolley (a plank, four pram wheels and the luxury of rope steering). It was my job to bring two buckets of water a day for drinking. Two old ladies offered me sixpence if I would do the same for them. I did this twice, but on the second trip, the water had been turned back on for two hours a day and so I sat at home, waited a while, and then made my delivery which had come from our tap. This is how fortunes are made, I thought. Sadly, I never got another order because I think they found out the water was back on for part of the day and soon got wise. The water may have been on for two hours a day, but the trouble was that you did not know when. My Mum used to keep all the pans and buckets at the ready, including the bath tap on and the plug in. We came home one day and, as we walked in, we saw the water coming down the stairs like rapids. Mum ran into the kitchen thinking she could turn the water off. She switched on the light by the door (it was one of the old type made of brass). Six feet away was the sink with a brass tap still running. The electric flash jumping from switch to tap was terrific. Fortunately, Mum did not even get a shock.

She sent me off to get Grandad from a couple of streets away to bring his turnkey. After turning off the water at the mains, he ran up stairs to let the water out of the bath. For some reason, our bathroom had a two-inch high wooden threshold in it and as he stepped inside, his slippers filled with cold water up to his ankles. We thought he was going to have a heart attack, but once he got over the shock, the day was saved.

BOMBED OUT IN THE BLITZ

by Margaret Parsons

I remember swinging to and fro on the garden gate. It was 1939 and I was four, the second youngest of five children living in the London suburbs. News came that we were at war with Germany. My parents grew anxious and became worried. They had already been through one war and Dad had seen his brother killed in France and had been gassed himself in the trenches, along with many of his comrades. Nevertheless, he joined the ARP and became a road warden giving help where it was needed. Then the bombs started to fall and we all had to have Anderson shelters built in our gardens. These were a novelty at first; the large dug-out covered by corrugated iron and earth with a set of steps leading inside. We loved going into them. They smelt earthy and dusty and to sleep on bunks either side was a new experience for us children. The air raid warning would go and we would trudge down into this earthy space mostly at night and half asleep. When the all clear went we would clamber out to see the red skies and smoke as London burned. Our planes flew overhead and fire engines wailed.

However the novelty began to wear off and we all grew tired and anxious to the extent that we could not be bothered to go outside in the cold winter months. One night we were sitting around the warm coal fire in the kitchen when the siren went. Then, suddenly the bombing started. Planes seemed to roar just above our heads and we all screamed. Mum quickly pulled us into the cupboard under the stairs. Not long afterwards, there was a tremendous thud and the house shook violently, then for a few seconds everything was eerily silent.

In complete darkness, the next thing we heard was the sounds of falling glass and roof tiles crashing down. Mum started shouting our names one by one and when my turn came I was kneeling on the floor. I tugged at her skirt but, in shock, could not utter a word. We realised that my sister, Betty, was not with us and Mum was frantic and kept calling her as we tried to get out. The situation, as chaotic as it was, was made much worse because the door would not budge. Suddenly, we heard Dad calling us. He had been on duty and had heard that one of the houses in our street had taken a direct hit and all the peopled had been killed outright. What must have gone through his mind as he dashed home!

Dad eventually scrambled through the wreckage, frantically clawing at the debris and managing to free the cupboard door, hauling us out one by one. On seeing him, Mum burst into tears with shock and the fear of what might have been. Suddenly, to everyone's great relief, little Betty appeared. She'd been hiding under our large wooden kitchen table and crept towards us. We were all overjoyed to see her and we shared hugs and kisses, overcome with emotion. Flames from the blast had blown across the room and we realised she could have easily been killed.

The house itself was wrecked; furniture broken, everything smashed, the roof tiles gone, windows out and doors off. There was thick dust hanging in the air and covering everything. The back garden was heaped with roof tiles. We ended up with blackened faces sitting in a pub at the end of the road and being given crisps and lemonade (a rare treat). Dad did go back to the house and tried to rescue an old mattress for us to sleep on, but I felt so scared and uneasy that, until exhaustion took over, I just stared into space and refused to talk because of the shock of it all.

We were eventually transported to a large civic hall with hundreds of other bombed out families where we stayed until we were re-housed, making do with little food, few toilets or washing facilities and sleeping on mattresses.

Fortunately, being a large family, we were given the vicar's requisitioned house on the outskirts of Wimbledon. The vicar had moved to his country residence for the duration of the war. This house was twice the size of ours and in a lovely road with a large garden, but to me it was spooky and, for many years, I would dream of ghosts walking along the long landing outside our bedroom. I then started school but with more air raids and sleepless nights, I did not learn much.

My elder sisters and brother were evacuated to Yapton in Sussex, but soon came home preferring to be with Mum and Dad. My younger sister (age five in 1942), who was a baby in arms when the war started, and I (age seven) were evacuated when the doodle bugs started being deployed. In fact, we had another near miss when one swooped down in front of the house and then dived up again to land on our local church, destroying it. We got away with a few smashed windows. So, two sad little girls were taken to Euston and then by train to Poynton, near Stockport, for what was to be a whole year (1942/43). We could not believe the lovely home we went to; the quiet fields opposite, the countryside and the views. No bombing here and no sleepless nights.

The couple we were then living with, the Woods, were an elderly, kindly couple and strong Methodists, but they had no children and found it hard to cope. I was sent before a board of people for being naughty. I have to laugh now, but to break a knitting needle while doing a handstand on an armchair was an unheard of offence. They did not seem to realise that me being made responsible for my sister, plus the constant worry of Mum and Dad facing danger all the time and not knowing what may happen in the future, was a frightening experience for a seven year old. They sent us to church three times every Sunday; C of E in the morning, Sunday school in the afternoon and Methodist church in the evenings. We had to walk a mile to and fro each time. When we started school, any spare time we had we were shut out to play in all weathers come rain or shine. We adjusted, however, and it did us no harm. The Woods clothed and fed us well, but when they said they would like to adopt my sister, Mum and Dad promptly came to get us. We came home two little healthy, well dressed and well-mannered children.

At the end of the war, the celebrations began. My elder sisters went up to Trafalgar Square like so many, to the amazing dancing, singing and celebrations. We younger ones and parents had street parties with everyone chipping in. There was a great sense of comradeship throughout the war years. We considered ourselves so lucky to have survived this terrible period.

THE WAY WE WERE

by Sheila Passmore

In 1922 when I was born, the roads were obviously less busy than today, but they still buzzed with a variety of vehicles. Coal was delivered in heavy hessian sacks by a flat-backed lorry drawn by two cart horses and, if the house had a cellar, tipped into a hole in the pavement (or somewhere else convenient) and between deliveries, covered with a heavy metal cover. Any manure left by the horses was quickly gathered up to fertilise the garden rhubarb or whatever. In the evening, a pony and trap carrying a couple of milk churns drove round the district – presumably to top up the morning supply which came in glass bottles very early on an electric float - we were often woken by its whining, whirring motor.

A handcart was used by our window cleaner and also by a rather old man who turned up occasionally pushing a cart laden with small flat fish known in our household as flukes and also referred to as dabs. I think he caught them locally off shore. Bread came in a large petrol-fuelled van fitted with shelves which slid out to reveal different sized loaves. Meat and fish were bought day by day because there were obviously no refrigerators, but our weekend joint was delivered by a teenaged boy who rode a bicycle fitted with a large metal basket over the front wheel. Newspaper delivery was on foot although some of the lads probably rode bikes.

Public transport was mainly provided by tram. In fact, Birkenhead was one of the first towns in the country to run a tram service. Some buses were used as early as the 1920s – double deckers and one or two single deckers. The trams were eventually displaced completely by buses. I can remember a gala evening when the last tram toured the town, illuminated and decked out in flags. They were real boneshakers and we were delighted with the comfort of the new vehicles.

Very few people owned motor cars. My grandparents had a pony and trap and my uncle drove a bull-nosed Morris throughout this period. Packed to capacity with children, sitting on the floor or each others laps, we travelled to some of the many beaches dotted around the Wirral coast. My earliest recollection of cars would be Fords such as seen in Laurel and Hardy films. In this period of a couple of decades, a greater variety of private cars – Armstrong Siddeley, Morris, Vauxhall and Jaguars became popular and I regularly saw, of all things, a Bugatti.

Most houses were lit by gas, which gave a clear bluish light. I can clearly remember its acid smell and hissing sound. My parents took over my grandparents' house just before I was born and had it wired, so I never actually lived solely with gas light. The mantle which provided the incandescence was made of very fragile material and needed constant replacement. There was always a switch at hand for me, but electricity was used only when strictly essential. We possessed only two electric appliances – an iron and a wireless (built from a kit, I seem to remember). Electric lighting was used very sparingly. My goodness, lights were never left on in an empty room! There were vacuum cleaners but the function was very poor. On one momentous occasion my mother borrowed her sister-in-law's, but decided that her Eubank carpet sweeper (pushed to and fro by hand) or even a stiff brush and dust pan were more efficient.

This was supposed to be an era of doors left unlocked and neighbours popping in and out to borrow cups of sugar. I don't remember anything like that. It was a depressed area during a depression, but I look back on what seemed then, and even now, in retrospect, a golden age for at least one small girl.

THE SHOCK OF MOVING TO ENGLAND

By Sandra Pope

I was born in Scotland in June, 1940, and we lived in the small town of Mauchline in Ayrshire. Our house was a large red sandstone building with a big back garden to play in and a small one at the front. My family consisted of Mum and Dad and two older brothers. We had lots of people around us because both parents came from a family of seven, so we were never short of company. They say that what you never had you don't miss, so never having had lots of sweets, or fruits like bananas, I certainly did not miss them. Life for me, therefore, was just fine.

So it came as a bit of a surprise when relatives started saying: 'So you're all off to England'. I was four years old by this time and thought England must be another town. Suddenly, strange things started to occur; we were told there would be no room for our big rocking horse or my beautiful dolls' pram and, unfortunately, they were given away. I'm sure my parents regretted this later as toys were unavailable for a long time after the war ended. I don't remember saying goodbye to everyone, either, but I understood we had to move because of dad's work.

We boarded the train in Kilmarnock on our journey to Crewe; Mum, Tom, Bill and me. The carriages were packed with servicemen and all the seats were taken. No one smiled or looked happy —all of them were just sitting smoking. I could not understand why no one offered my mum a seat. As I was little, I sat on the floor. My brothers read comics and we had a stand-up picnic along the way.

The first leg of our travels was to Carlisle and should have taken two and a half hours, but several delays on the line meant we arrived two hours late and so we missed our connection. A very kind porter took us to the ladies' waiting room and brought us tea and buns while we sat and waited. Then we were told the chilling news: the train we should have been on had been involved in an horrific crash and many people had been killed or injured. Thank God we missed it. But poor Dad, who was waiting at Crewe didn't know we weren't on it - there was no method of communication to tell him otherwise.

It took us hours to finally get to Crewe. We arrived at midnight and Dad, who by this time was frantic with worry, was overjoyed to see his tired little family re-united at last.

He had been able to find a rented house for us in Edleston Road. What a shock this new house was; not a warm, loving home like the one we'd left behind. This rented place was on a main road by traffic lights. We walked into our freezing new home and we kids were given a hot drink and bundled off to bed with hot water bottles. We lived there until our new house was built some 18 months later in Audlem Road, Nantwich.

HOW I DEFEATED A MONSTER HEDGE

by Geoff Pritchard

It is relatively easy to draw comparisons of life in the 1950s to the ways of today. Sixty years ago, you could walk out of work on a Friday evening and start a completely new job on the Monday. The Crewe Chronicle and the Evening Sentinel were packed with a variety of jobs; from farm labourer to accounts clerk, salesman to textile worker. The expectations of life were much simpler. My father was an engineer at Crewe railway works and had seen workers laid off in the 1930s. He'd been recruited by the LNWR (London North Western Railway) as an apprentice fitter before the First World War. He went to night school where he matriculated and was fortunate not to lose his job during the Depression, eventually becoming a foreman.

What is difficult to equate is the attitude towards life. As far as the average family was concerned, you worked to earn a living in order to eat, have a week's holiday and go to the pictures on Saturday night. Work was normally five full days a week plus a half day on Saturday. As foreman, Dad earned reasonable money. Mum's place of work was the house and family. Washday was always on a Monday and took around seven hours to complete, plus drying and ironing time. She never had a washing machine in which she could put the dirty clothing, press a button, then watch television for a few hours.

We didn't possess a car until Dad was well into his fifties. We each had a bicycle and that was a perfectly good enough method of transport. Dad had the same principles as most of his contemporaries: 'If you haven't got the cash you can't have it'. Would our nation have been better off if they'd listened to my dad? Yes, I say. When we look back now, I am so grateful that I was brought up along these same lines.

As a youngster I went to Sunday school and looked forward to the annual outing to Rhyl. But I had to work in order to get some spending money. One year when I was about 14, Dad told me he'd give me ten shillings if I lowered 'that hedge' to a height of six feet. The hedge in question divided our garden from a farmer's drive where he used to drive his cows down twice a day to a shippon. It was a mixture of holly and hawthorn, eight feet high, three feet thick and 120 feet long. It was more than a challenge. I needed a saw, step ladders, a pair of shears and long-handled pruners. No such thing as electrical or petrol-powered cutters then, of course, but I was not going to be beaten.

Even though my mates called on me for football, this hedge took priority. It was a warm summer so I thought it would be rather 'cissy' of me to protect my hands with gloves, or my arms with a jersey. So I cut and I slashed and I sawed. I reckoned I could just about complete the job in the six weeks before the trip. My arms were covered in scratches and changed colour to orange as iodine was unmercifully smeared on them most days. The tweezers and a needle were used after each session to remove the thorns that became embedded in my hands and arms with the odd one or two in my legs.

In the end I completed the job, but with only a few days to spare. I stood back, looked at 'that hedge' and said: 'There … I've beaten yer.'

I was delighted when Dad gave me the ten bob note, but not nearly so much as when he said something perhaps out of character. 'Well done son, I'm proud of you.'

Did I enjoy my day in Rhyl? Yes I did. But I didn't go mad with the money. I'd worked too hard to waste it on those slot machines. It was one of those lessons in life that you look back on. It helped me realise the value of money – and it gave me a sense of achievement. Only recently I passed our old cottage. 'That hedge' is still there – but it had recently been layered. I doubt if whoever did it got nearly as much out of it as I did.

COPING WITH SNOW, ICE – AND WAR

by Dot Roxby

It was 1940 and I might as well have been born in the Arctic. There was snow and ice everywhere - as well as a war raging around us. My mother told me that everything was difficult in the icy weather. We had no electricity, only a coal-fired small range and a gas water heater. There was no heating upstairs, no bathroom or inside toilet and only a scullery at the top of the cellar steps. At least the cellar 'meat safe' kept the food pretty cool and the flies away.

Our toilet was across the shared yard. There were three houses and three toilets which tended to freeze up in winter as did those at school. I once slipped on the ice at school going to the toilet and sustained a nasty cut over my eye. The scar is under my eyebrow which I have never had plucked. The weekly wash took place in the wash house, also across the yard from our back door. We had a copper boiler, which had to be filled on a Monday, a posser, and a mangle. We used dolly blue to keep things white. Another day was ironing day.

My mother was a great baker so we had lots of good food, managed with a very small budget. This was especially true when my father was fighting with the troops across Europe and we struggled on a soldier's pay. Mother had been a secretary/pa to a wool firm in Bradford, dealing with the purchase of merino wool from places including Australia and Spain. She spoke some French and, I think, some Spanish. She was sacked in 1937 because she got married. Married women were not allowed to work at the time. My father was a management accountant in a textiles firm based in Manchester and Leeds. This was in the days when such accountants were rated way below chartered accountants and this was reflected in their earnings.

One of my first memories is of having to get under the table during an air raid. We usually went into the cellar, so this particular raid cannot have been a 'close one'. We were in a village between cities, so we did not have any big raids. We did have a prisoner of war camp in the woods which, I think, housed Italians. At the end of our street was a small road called Back Lane. At its end was a council yard where the horses were kept. We suffered with a lot of flies and I remember some big nasty horseflies. We had to go and collect the manure from the lane to put on our gardens. Back Lane was also great for cycling on when we were learning to balance on two wheels.

I remember my childhood as a very happy one. We went blackberrying along the hedgerows. Our next door neighbours and their dog went with me once. I was about five and I got told off because I picked all the big easy ones! We children wandered the field paths and, in that dreadful winter of 1947, we sledged down the hills when nothing else could move along the snowdrift-blocked roads. The milkman must have got though somehow, though. He poured our milk out of a big can into our containers. We always knew someone who had TB but we didn't know it was linked to non-pasteurised milk. I had lots of friends in the village, at church and at school and everyone knew everyone else. You could not get away with anything as a child. I am very grateful for my loving caring family and the safety I knew that protected me from the realities of the wartime struggle to survive. We only had the radio to tell us what was going on and the news brought back by my father and others when they came home on leave. My sister, who was born in 1943, did not know who our father was when he came home permanently in 1947 after demob. I still have his Royal Artillery jacket and I can clearly remember his kitbag, which travelled back and forth with him.

When my Grandmother died, we moved to live with Grandad to look after him. I think it must have been very difficult for everyone. The house was crowded with five people and three bedrooms, but it did have a nice big bathroom and a narrow ergonomic kitchen. This was much better for us, but poor Grandad wanted to listen to classical music on the radio while we wanted *Children's Hour*. He had to get rid of most of his lovely mahogany furniture because it was too big. A house clearer came and took lots of lovely things away and probably paid little. We had to walk much further to school every day. It must have been a mile or more each way. The buses were good although I do not remember using them much except to go about three miles to the dentist.

We had a week's holiday every year around 1948 and we always went on CHA holidays. They were really good because we enjoyed the walks and the company. On Bank Holidays, a steam train came to the station and lots of people from the village had a day out in the Yorkshire Dales. Our Sunday school annual trip also went by train and sometimes by coach. During the next decade, we acquired three 'life-changing' items; electricity, a Twin Tub washing machine, then a fridge. Later, we also got a small family car and I passed my driving test at the age of 17. I don't ever remember going out in the car without one of my parents, however, as it was their car. As a student, I was obviously more independent, and I made some exciting rail journeys across France and around Scandinavia. In the 1960s, we welcomed television, bigger fridges and more opportunities to travel and acquire possessions. This rapid change has continued ever since as lifestyles have changed along with increased purchasing power.

SPITFIRES CHASING THEIR QUARRY

by Gordon Roxby

Air raid shelters stood row upon row in our schoolyard. Shaped like submarines with a conning tower at one end, they were covered in earth and grass and had a set of steps stretching down between blast walls at the other end. Inside, two wooden slatted benches and an iron ladder went up the conning tower to a metal hatch for fast escape. During one air raid on Merseyside, the whole street seemed to have taken shelter. Worried mothers watched anxiously as a group of older boys continually climbed the ladder pretending they were going outside. This is my earliest memory. I was two years old.

Searchlights would wave in the sky. If one lit up an aircraft, other searchlights would join it to make a cone of light and then the anti-aircraft guns would open up. Next morning, the older boys would search for pieces of shrapnel which had rained down and were now to be kept as souvenirs. Barrage balloons were dotted here and there carrying thick cables to slice into any stray enemy aircraft. The River Mersey had a multitude of them, soaring over their barges moored on the water. Later in the war, our house had an air raid shelter built in its backyard with brick walls and a reinforced concrete roof. The Ack-Ack gun emplacements remained long after the war was over.

My native town is Ellesmere Port. Nearby, and to the west, was Hooton Aerodrome where Spitfires were based. On one occasion a lone German bomber flew over our street chased by three Spitfires. It was shot down shortly afterwards. 'What are those white lines in the sky?' I once asked my father. 'They are aeroplanes' he explained. Spitfires could fly high enough to make vapour trails. When I was three, my father took me and my baby sister to see Tiger Moth training aircraft flying into a small landing field at Little Sutton on 'circuit and bumps'. On another occasion a soldier came home down our street. Our street gang of mainly little boys asked him: 'How many Germans have you killed?' He said: 'None.' So we left him.

The Home Guard practiced in our school playground which was at the bottom of our road. Our town was a port on the Manchester Ship Canal. Ships from the Atlantic Convoys berthed there. American sailors toured the town. We greeted them cheekily with: 'Got any gum, chum?' An American sea captain was very taken by me and my sister, then aged about four and two, out walking with our Dad. We were dressed in smart oatmeal coats and hats made by our mum who was a seamstress. With Dad's permission he took our photograph and then sent us copies back from the States. The photo has an air raid shelter sign in the background. The shelter was the very large cellar of The Station Inn. He later sent us boxes of chocolates, chewing gum and even swimming costumes.

A large American air-base was set up at Burtonwood, near Warrington. We could watch large numbers of planes rising into the sky, circling and forming into large squares. They were silver and sparkled in the sunlight. The squares would then fly away to bomb Germany, part of the 1,000 bomber raids. Years later, I asked a war historian why war films showed these bombers in dark camouflage paint, yet I remembered them as shining in the sunlight. 'Your memory is correct.' I was told. 'The planes usually only lasted a fortnight before being shot down and it wasn't worthwhile painting them.'

I mention these wartime memories because to us kids this was normal life – being bombed or bombing, people trying to kill us or our side trying to kill the enemy. Even our cinemas with the children's Saturday matinees were about cowboys killing cowboys (goodies and baddies) or about cowboys killing Indians. There were bomb sites around the town. Each street had its own little gang of juniors who played out on the streets and became close friends. Occasionally one would raid another gang's territory throwing 'half house bricks' collected from bomb sites. There was a lot of shouting and throwing at a distance with no injuries but lots of tall stories. Street crazes would appear and, suddenly, we were on roller skates or racing in our own soap box derby or playing whip and tops, with tops of all shapes spinning for minutes at a time. Our whips were made out of bamboo canes and thick string. By flicking them we could make the whips 'crack' with a loud noise.

133

Shopping was a daily trip that took a long time. Groceries were usually bought from Dyson's across the road. We had to queue twice, once on the bacon counter and once on the grocery counter. Bacon was sliced while you waited. Butter was patted into blocks, sugar poured into bags - all in front of each and every customer. Greengroceries were from a Meredith on the corner of our road. Just round the corner was the butcher's and further along, shoe repairers, a fresh fish shop, a noisy pub and then Woolworths. Within about a hundred yards was the Co-op. Here, they paid out 'divi' once or twice a year. Ration books were normal and we could only buy certain items with coupons. Meat and other perishables were stored in a 'safe' mainly to keep the flies at bay. This was a small wooden-framed cupboard with metal mesh. The milk cart was drawn by a knowledgeable horse that stopped outside the right houses. The milk was ladled from the urn into jugs brought out from the houses. We all had gas masks, too, and I still remember their rubbery smell. Our new baby brother, Gerald, had a full body gas mask shaped like a cradle with a top lid.

Dad's job was in an iron works walking on very hot metal floors. Any water falling on the floor immediately boiled off. Iron shod clogs were the only possible foot wear. He made his own clogs and also pairs for us. He taught us how to make them and I can still remember how. We could make sparks with them as we walked. The iron works had no canteen so we used to walk to the works gates with mum who carried a metal tea canteen and also his hot stew lunch in a small basin suspended in a red polka-dot handkerchief.

Mum was a seamstress and had worked at Browns of Chester. In later years Browns was bought by Debenhams. She had had to leave work before the war because she got married. However she owned a Jones Treadle sewing machine so made most of our clothes, also dresses for the women in our street. It was a common sight to see dress patterns laid out on the table or the floor. Dad always complained that she never charged her customers enough for her work.

Toilet paper was newspapers torn into rough squares. Beds were warmed with either a pottery type vinegar bottle filled with hot water or a metal plate taken from the oven in the fire range and wrapped in an old blanket. On the railway station I was intrigued by the rusted up chocolate dispensing machines which I was told by the older children had bars of real chocolate in them 'pre-war'. 'Pre-war' was a golden age which we had lost altogether. Born three weeks before the outbreak, I was very proud of being 'pre-war'.

Mum, Dad, me and my younger sister, June, and my brother, Gerald, lived in a rented terraced house, built around 1900. It had a small front garden. Downstairs there was a vestibule, hallway, a parlour, living room and kitchen. Upstairs there were three bedrooms and a bathroom with a toilet. It also had a loft. The backyard led to a wash house, a toilet and a coal house. Facing the coal house was our air raid shelter. A back gate led into the cobbled back entry. The coal house was stocked with coal, coke and wood. By the age of five or six we were skilled at chopping wood into fire sticks for lighting the fire. If wood was short, we made spills to light the fires. Spills were newspapers rolled up and then wound round into tight rings. One winter, perhaps 1947, there was no coal, so we used to go to the gas works with a hand trolley lent by the greengrocer and buy a sack of coke. After some weeks there was no more coke so we picked scraps of coke from a local gas works dumping area. Bath night came and for a few weeks all three of us were bathed in the dolly tub with water heated on the gas ring. We also collected logs using a bow saw from nearby Stanney Woods.

The wash house had a corner copper i.e. a huge bowl built into brick walls with a fire underneath. This was used to boil the washing. Other equipment included a wash tub, a dolly peg, a posser and a mangle. The fire under the copper was lit on a Monday and the clothes and sheets were washed or boiled. After going through the mangle the clothes were hung out to dry on a long washing line Monday and Tuesday hopefully to dry. A clothes rack hanging from the living room ceiling completed the drying. Ironing day was usually Wednesday with some items going back on the rack overnight. Irons were heated on the gas rings or on the fire range. The invention of the modern domestic washing machine has done more to change people's lives than almost any other device.

Households were sometimes historically defined by their hearths or cooking fires. During the war our hearth was a small cooking

135

range. It had a fire, a hob, an oven and perhaps a warming area. It was surrounded on the floor in a fender designed to stop falling coals from reaching the rug or carpet. It heated a back boiler for the hot water, too. The fire was great for toasting bread with a toasting fork and for roasting chestnuts. The range was cleaned carefully and regularly using Zebo liquid poured onto a duster and then later polished. In those years everyone burnt coal or coke. The coal man delivered to every house. All chimneys emitted lots of smoke and fog was frequent in winter with visibility sometimes down to five to 10 yards. Over time, all buildings especially old public buildings became black with soot from the chimneys. Other callers to the street were the binmen, the rag and bone man and the fish man with his barrow. Another regular cleaning job was the front path and doorsteps using a donkey stone. Eventually the old range went and was replaced by a modern tiled fireplace.

We had a large valve radio in the living room. The aerial was a long wire stretching down the backyard to a high pole. Our house had once been struck by lightning and to prevent this happening again there was a swing switch near the radio which could isolate the aerial during a thunderstorm. Sometime in the 1950s we acquired a piano and also a record player for 78rpm records. Richer friends nearby had radiograms. Our first television and washing machine would have arrived about 1960.

Street games were normal for us when we were not at school. Only two cars were ever parked in our road, so the street belonged to the children. Seasonal games included May Queens for the girls. They sang:

'A May Day a May Day
The birds began to sing,
A song we never shall forget
Repeated in the alpha bet
A May Day a May Day'

Girls played ball games against a wall with a variety of singing rhymes. They also collected and exchanged beads. There was also 'conkers' and collecting wood for bonfires. This included raids on

136

neighbouring bonfires for material. Our bonfires were lit in the middle of the road. After the frightening explosions of the war, I was terrified of fireworks. Leap frog and leaping on a row of children's backs to touch a wall. What was that game called? We had chasing games including tick and 'Alley Alley Oh'. I have seen a skipping rope across the street and children and adults in it together. We played football using coats for goal post and wickets drawn in chalk on a wall for cricket. My father often supervised cricket games to keep them running smoothly because there was invariably a dispute whether the 'wicket' had been hit or not. Eventually, street games were killed off by television and by the increase in traffic. A culture going back centuries was lost to the streets although a recent TV broadcast found it still alive in primary school playgrounds. Other leisure pursuits in the 1940s were picnics, with sandwiches made at the picnic place, and swimming in wonderful 1930s Rivacre Swimming Pool. On the larger scale, coach trips were arranged by Mrs Bainbridge for our street to Blackpool once or twice a year.

Other entertainment came from several cinemas showing the same film from Mondays to Wednesdays, followed by a different programme from Thursdays to Saturdays. Sundays had a programme all its own for the day.

Each autumn our family collectively pickled shallots and red cabbage for the winter. Family-wise, we also went on walks. Dad and Mum were wonderful entertainers and there always seemed to be something interesting up ahead even if it was the wording on a pavement grid or the strange chimney pots on a house. We children learned curiosity for the extraordinary in the ordinary things of life. Dad was always extending our childhood experiences with such things as visits to ship's engine rooms in the docks and a tour of his iron works. Ellesmere Port was a hub for the Shropshire Union Canal and the Manchester Ship Canal. Horses still pulled some barges on the 'Shroppie' during the war. There was a customs house and some giant flour mills.

After the war, Dad left the iron works to work for a few years at an Admiralty dump, and then at Shell Oil company's Thornton Research Centre where he became a printer on lithography machines. Our smallish street, Exeter Road, led down to Ellesmere Port Town's

137

Football Club which played in the Cheshire League and attracted crowds of 2,000 to 4,000. We followed them in away matches to towns across Cheshire and North Wales. My father was a friend of Joe Mercer, who played for Town and had married the grocer's daughter from the shop across from our house. Mercer, of course, went on to a distinguished soccer career, playing for Everton and Arsenal and managing several top clubs. Dad also knew another local lad who made good – the famous Wolves and England player, Stan Cullis.

In our teens in the 1950s, most churches ran large youth clubs and teenagers had innocent temporary romances lasting a few weeks. Later in the 1950s we went dancing in Chester or Liverpool. Some of the greats were around such as Johnny Dankworth and Chris Barber. One highlight was going to the Liverpool Philharmonic to hear Jack Teagarden and Ella FitzGerald. I built radios and nearly became a radio ham on shortwave radio.

My education was totally free. This included university in London (and living in Bloomsbury) and Theological College. The latter two were on Cheshire State Scholarships. I had to work in the holidays, but we had no student loans then - all fees and all accommodation paid.

Living conditions steadily improved in Britain from 1945 until the present when most households have better situations than Royalty two hundred years ago.

CREWE TOWN'S THREE Rs

by Barrie Ryder

I was born at 68 Hope Street, Crewe, on the 14th April 1937, the 25th anniversary of the collision of the *Titanic* with an 'inconsiderate' iceberg. I was the seventh child of Albert and Annie Ryder (nee Tilley) having two elder brothers, followed by four girls. From an historic point of view, 68 Hope Street, had a brick and concrete air raid shelter which is still there today as part of the rear extension. My eldest brother, Derek, who died in 2002, wrote some lovely memories of our family. It is a commendable piece of social history which I have had the pleasure of using in a delivery to our U3A local history group and several other organisations.

I went to three schools: Pedley Street Infants, now the railway police building, Bedford Street Juniors, now a housing estate, and Crewe County Grammar School in Ruskin Road, now the Ruskin Sports College. I left school at 16 with four GCEs. In those days, Crewe had two industries – the railways and Rolls-Royce, which you could say was the town's three Rs. My girlfriend's father was one of the bosses on the railway so I plumped for that, obtaining a post in the Traffic Control as an assistant controller.

From January 1956 to January 1958 I did my National Service as a company clerk for "C" Company, the Cheshire Regiment – something I have talked about to members of the U3A local history group. My CO was Major Peter Lawrence de Carteret Martin who became a general - what a wonderful name and what a wonderful person! My other main memory of this time was an eight-month stint in Berlin, then a similar period in Barnard Castle, Co. Durham. Next came four months at Litchfield and four months in Luneberg, Germany, where Monty took the surrender of Admiral Doenitz on Luneberg Heath in 1945. I saw the commemorative stone 'in situ' which, I believe, is now at Sandhurst.

The first ever steam locomotive in Germany came from the UK and was unloaded by a wooden crane at Luneberg from the river

Elbe. In fact the crane is still there. I also met a German family in those four months who treated me like a son – Walter and Lisle Schneider, a middle aged couple, with three daughters. On one of my evening visits, Walter had tuned in to Sputnik 1, the world's first artificial Earth satellite. The Russian craft sent out radio pulses, which were picked up as steady 'beeps' from outer space by amateur radio operators throughout the world. What a thrill that was as it sped round the Earth at 18,000 miles an hour, heralding the start of the 'space race.'

I returned to civilian life in January 1958 and took up my job again, gaining promotion to a class one controller, still in my late twenties. But I wasn't content. By this time I had a very nice semi at Haslington, two kids and a car. Ten years earlier I'd thought that cars were only for the well-off. Now I'd got it all! But the job became boring and I left the railway, bought an empty shop and for five years didn't know where the next housekeeping was coming from. Success came eventually and I have had a good life in what future generations may well call the Golden Age.

COD LIVER OIL & MALT – DELICIOUS

by Mim Ryder

Writing my memories is something I had been thinking about for quite a while, but like many things, didn't get around to. Well, a wet Cornish weekend comes in quite handy sometimes! Hence this is how my memories of childhood until the age of 15 came about. I was born to Reginald Stanley Cliffe and Florence Ellen Cliffe, nee Gregory, on 25th October 1945, the youngest of four children, two of each. My father was the second eldest of 13 children, and had quite a hard childhood. They moved house many times to accommodate the ever-growing family. His last house was a former manse in Herdman Street, Crewe. His father had moved to Crewe from Eccleshall, Staffs, in the late 1890s to join the railway as an engine driver. He married my grandmother in 1900, and then went off to the Boar War. His name is on the memorial in Crewe Park. Granny Cliffe originated from Lincolnshire, a daughter of the headmaster at South Kelsey School. When Dad left school, he took up an apprenticeship as a lather boy. He had to leave this job as it wasn't bringing in enough money to help the family. He then got a job on the railway, and became an engine driver like his father.

Mother had a totally different upbringing. Youngest of two girls, she lived with her family in Coppenhall on a smallholding belonging to her parents. Her father, Grandad Gregory came from Winsford and, apart from running the holding, worked full time in Crewe Works as a riveter in the boiler shop, eventually becoming the charge-hand. Granny Gregory also originated from Winsford. Mother's elder sister was allowed to take a job working for the Co-op, but Mother was made to stay at home and help around the house and the holding. This arrangement really angered Mother as she would have loved to have got out meeting people.

I believe I was quite small as a baby and that I could fit into a two-pint jug. My first 'cot' was the top draw of the built-in set, to the side of the living room chimney breast. But, of course, we didn't call it the 'living-room' then as it was better known as the kitchen. My parents didn't own the house but rented it off the Crewe Borough Council as it was then. Mum and Dad were quite proud of our home and kept it really nice. It was a three-bedroomed semi with gardens front and back. In those days I could name every neighbour living in the street; we all got on and helped each other when necessary. As with any community of that time, we had a neighbour, Mrs Cheetham, who 'laid out the dead' and helped at births until the district nurse arrived.

The living room (kitchen) didn't have carpet. Initially we had a pegged rug, which we as a family pegged. Cutting up old coats or other suitable material was used. I can feel the sore fingers now from the cutting. We measured along a piece of wood which Dad had cut and made smooth to ensure all the pieces were of the same length. The backing material was made from hessian sacks, cut open and washed prior to use, then sewn together. As time went on, a piece of coconut matting was laid with the red tiled floor around it and 'red raddled' (Cardinal red polish) and polished to make it really shiny. This may have made the room cosier, but boy did it hurt your knees when playing!

Suspended from the ceiling was the clothes rack, a great asset, apart from the washing hanging in front of your face at times! The fire grate had an oven and hob to one side and a coal fire in the grate. I cannot remember my mother using the oven or hob for cooking. The oven was a great place to warm your clothes on a cold morning, also great for melting the rubber button on my liberty bodice! Each week there would be a cup of senna pod infusing in the hob section ready for Friday night. Getting the fire to burn at times was a challenge so the shovel was stood up at the front with a piece of paper laid across it to make it 'draw' better. I lost count how many times the paper caught fire in the process. I also remember on some occasions sugar would be thrown on to encourage it to burn. Obviously, this would be after rationing was over. Mother used to like painting this grate. It changed colour quite often. I can remember one of the colour schemes was a light green background with pink stippling on. Stippling? She would roll a piece of net curtain up into a ball and gently dip it into the pink paint, quite effective really. We

142

owned an upright piano. Goodness knows where that came from; there was no way my parents could have afforded to buy it. I can only think that my Granny Gregory bought it.

Our three-piece suite was a brown leatherette type, the dining table was a square shape, and I can remember mother spending hours polishing this - her pride and joy. Our back kitchen was a stark place to someone of pre-school age. The unplastered walls were painted a glossy green colour – gosh, horrible! In the corner was a copper boiler with a fire underneath. This was great for keeping us warm and, when not in use, we had to rely on a paraffin stove. The gas stove was grey enamel with curvy legs. In the corner by the window was the kitchen sink which was a brown 'slop stone' held up at one end by a brick wall. The draining board was white enamel. Being the person he was, Dad made a bench seat to accommodate the kids. I remember this being roughly four feet long, padded and covered in a red leatherette material. In later years the boiler was removed and a coke burning stove put in. The coke was got from the gas works in Wistaston Road. Dad used to push me in his home-made truck there to fill it with coke you could buy. It was great fun, except that there was no room for me on the way home. The Gas works was also a sinister place back in the 1950s and, for a shilling they would gas any unwanted pet.

I shared a bedroom with my sister. It was a double bed with a shaky up mattress which was okay when the bed linen had been changed and the mattress shaken, otherwise we just rolled into the middle. My two brothers shared a bed, too, one with a cast iron head and foot board. My youngest brother, Peter, and I used to have great fun playing on this bed as it was quite high up. Our favourite game was pretending it was a ship and we were surrounded by crocodiles. We had a bathroom, but no inside toilet. The toilet was situated at the back of the house. An inside toilet was put in by the council in the late Fifties. Our loo paper was old railway running time tables which hung from a hook on the back of the lavatory door. I got quite good at knowing the stops and timing from Crewe to Euston. Not only that, but the ink didn't rub off like newspaper!

Friday night was bath night. In winter, a zinc bath was brought into the kitchen in front of the fire (the bathroom being much too cold). As well as bath night it was the day to take the weekly medicine, Scott's emulsion. It was disgusting stuff that I can still smell now - it made me heave. Syrup of figs or Senna pods had to be taken as well; it was believed then that a good clear out of the system once a week was good for you. The only daily medicine I enjoyed was cod liver oil and malt, delicious!

My first few years up to starting school at five are vague. I do remember needing my tonsils out before school age. This was done at the Crewe Memorial Hospital. Dad took me; mother suffered from agoraphobia for many years. We got to the hospital too early so Dad took me for a walk around Crewe Park and bought an ice cream which was a rare treat. Hospital rules were very strict in those days, however, and parents weren't allowed to stay despite your young age. Oh how I cried!

Going to Sunday school was quite popular and 'normal' back then. One thing we looked forward to was going on the Sunday school trips, usually Prestatyn, Rhyl, or Southport. Having a new dress for the Church anniversary from Gordon's dress shop in Market Street was a big event. Each year I had a different colour.

My first school was The Bluebell Nursery near to St Michael's Church, Ford Lane Crewe. In earlier years the Bluebell Inn stood on that spot. A public path ran alongside the old pub where the story goes that someone was murdered down there. I think it was my second day at the nursery when I decided I would like to go home for my cocoa, which I always had after lunchtime while enjoying *Listen With Mother* on the radio. I can see myself now crawling on my hands and knees past the teacher and escaping. I recall it being a foggy day and running through the Coppenhall churchyard. When I arrived home it must have dawned on me that I had done something wrong. I crept into the house and hid under the living room table. My mother was not amused when she found me. She was also very annoyed that I hadn't been stopped by the school from escaping. I don't know how I knew my way home as it wasn't an area I was used to, and I certainly was not allowed to wander away from home at anytime.

After the nursery, I went to the infants/junior schools in Broad Street, Crewe. One of the years in junior school had to be spent in a railway carriage on the grounds of the North Street Methodist Church. It was quite fun really and I remember it felt cosy. School holidays were fun. For two weeks, I holidayed with my Aunty Lizzie and Uncle Albert Buckley on their farm in Minshull Vernon. I had jobs to do; one was collecting eggs from the hen house – something I wasn't keen on. I used to run around the shed and bang on the sides to make the hens scatter so I could go in and not be attacked. There were always a couple of broody hens in there giving me the beady eye and frightening me to death. Carrying buckets of milk up from the shippon to the dairy was hard work and spilling any was not allowed. Later in the morning, I used to walk down Eardswick Lane to a row of cottages to deliver their milk, in cans. Uncle Albert also taught me how to roll out the milk churns to the front of the farm ready for collection.

Christmas was a busy time on the farm although I wasn't struck on how Uncle Albert despatched the chickens. They had to be killed and plucked ready for the customers and I watched him cut their throats several times. On the other hand, haymaking time was great fun – especially playing in the hay barn and tasting Aunty Lizzie's delicious lemonade which she brought out for the men. Uncle Albert and I used to go off mushrooming in what he called the bottom field. One year he allowed me to drive the tractor, standing up. I was sworn to secrecy not to let Aunty Lizzie know as he would be in bother. He was great fun and I always remember him having a woodbine hanging from his lips which, magically, never fell out – even when he was talking. He also spoke in a broad Cheshire accent which was brilliant. In their farmhouse was a large pantry. To get inside, you had to go down three stone steps to where it was very cool. Butter, brawn, ham, cheese, and all sorts of jams were stored or made down there. The smell was lovely.

The Women's Institute held their meeting in the chapel schoolroom next to the farm. If one was on at the time of my holiday, then I got to go. I was also included in any trips that were being arranged by them. Aunty Lizzie & Uncle Albert were also caretakers of the chapel. I was allowed to go in and tinker on the piano or have a bash at the organ (Barrie & I got married at this chapel in 1992 and I am the secretary of the church now). The chapel used to have regular jumble sales. This was another thing which I was encouraged to get involved in and came in very handy for new clothes for me. At anniversary time and at Christmas, members of the church went out singing around the local farms; this was lovely except when we went to Hole House Farm where the Broads lived. In the farmyard they had dozens of geese. I'd rather face a pack of dogs than those vicious creatures!

During school holidays back at home, we always had things to do. I can't remember the word 'bored' ever being mentioned. Making our annual trolley cart was always done at our house with Dad supplying the parts and letting us build it ourselves.

May Day was always fun but very serious. One of the girls from our street would be selected to be the 'May Queen'. She would be dressed up in whatever we could get hold of that looked posh! Very often this would be a set of old net curtains draped around her with some sort of headgear, mainly old bead necklaces, begged or borrowed from parents. The trolley became the Queen's coach. We fastened a chair to the cart and draped it in material. Our Queen would sit, looking regal and important and we seemed to be out for hours parading up and down the street. I bet our parents laughed their heads off.

Roller skating was another favourite game, also whip and top. The tops were decorated with different coloured chalk. We played rounders across the width of the street with four gateposts being the home bases. Skipping was with a long washing line, a long enough rope for several of you to skip in together. French skipping using two ropes was also a favourite. There was a lamp post quite near to my house which had an arm sticking out near the top and an old bike tyre would be slung around the arm so we could swing from it. This had to be taken down at the end of the day because the grown-ups said it looked untidy. No one called us hooligans, just kids being kids and having fun. In the cricket season, out came the bats and balls with constant warnings not to hit the ball high because of the windows. Back then if a ball went into someone's garden we always politely knocked on the door to ask for it back. There's always one person in the street who wasn't quite so pleasant. That was Mr Jackson, a

146

special constable. I think you would call him a 'Jobsworth' now. They had no children.

When the Coronation came about several families were invited to go to Mr and Mrs Smith's house to watch it on their television as no one else had one. What a magical day it turned out to be. She had made lots of cakes and we had a really good party. The TV was only tiny with a large magnifying glass in front. Having no children of their own, the Smiths were always very kind to the neighbourhood kids - not like the previous-named person.

As I got older, I was allowed to go off up Mclaren Street to call for friends. Across from their house was the 'Bricky Pit'. What a playground of fun that was - and dangerous, too, which made it all the more interesting. It had a large pit of deep water left over from the brickwork days. To one side of the pit was a steep lime slop which came down to about four feet from the water. We used to slide down it on whatever we could find on the land fill to sit on, stopping right up to the water's edge. We also fished in there with our nets, catching massive stickleback fish. Also flying around during the summertime were large beautiful dragonflies. The lads used to swim in the pit, but it was too smelly and dirty for me. One boy actually died as a result of playing there. The rumour was that he had caught something from the dirty water and that had killed him. I think most of old Crewe is buried under this area of ground, now a green space with an astroturf area and still to this day is enjoyed by many.

In fact, this landfill site also became very handy for bicycle spares. My first bicycle, a Christmas present, I now know was made up from spares my Dad had collected from there. I loved that bike. Painted totally black, even the wheels, to cover up the rust I suspect, but I didn't care. No one in the street minded either as they all wanted to take 'turns' riding it.

Dad also made us a swing which hung from a beam in the old guards van we had as a shed in Cliffe Road. This was great fun. One of my favourite tricks was to hold onto the swing ropes then tip myself upside down and hang by my toes from the beam. Another pastime was walking on stilts, made by my brothers or our father. One year my eldest brother thought it a good idea to make a very large pair. Well, you could only get on them by climbing on to the shed first. Of course, I couldn't resist the temptation to have a go. I managed a few steps before the inevitable happened and, fortunately, I landed safely. If my Mother had been there, goodness knows what she would have said.

Crewe's Mclaren Street was better known as the 'Black Boards'. In fact I had no idea it was called Mclaren Street. I can only assume that it got its name from the boards which ran along its length to Evans Street from Underwood Lane because they were painted in dark creosote. It was a rough road with large pot holes and didn't get a proper surface until the later Fifties when they built bungalows along it. One of the fields nearby had a brilliant pond which iced over very thickly in the winter months and became our skating pond. The same field also held a fairground on it at times.

I mentioned earlier that we owned a piano. Peter, Jen and I all had piano lessons. Regretfully this didn't come too much. I suppose I succeeded the furthest as I actually took an examination, which I failed by one point. My exam piece was *The Blue Danube*. Mrs Wareham, our tutor, was very strict. When your fingers roamed to the incorrect key she would tap your knuckles with the ruler she always held. She had one of those metronomes on the top of the piano and it scared me to death.

Father was able to mend our school shoes. His youngest brother, Edgar, was a shoemaker. His shop was in Alton Street and he used to pass on odd bits of leather which Dad could use. We had several different sizes of last in the shed. One year, Dad showed me how to sole and heal a shoe. I was quite a tomboy really and liked getting my hands dirty. Going down to Granny and Grandad Gregory's place in Parkers Road was also an adventure. Grandad used to keep several beehives in one orchard which I found fascinating. He would be in there with his net hat on, string tied round his coat sleeves. The smoker, something like a metal jug/kettle with bellows at the handle, would be bellowing out. This made the bees dormant and he was able to check inside the hive or, when the honeycombs were ready for extracting the honey, he could remove them without too much hassle. Mind you, he did get stung a good few times and he always applied a dab of Dolly Blue onto the sting which did the trick. His honey was well regarded throughout south Cheshire and I still remember that lovely smell of recently-extracted honey.

He won most of the first prizes at the Crewe Carnival. Having two large orchards, fruit picking was also a busy time. We used to hang a string-handled sack bag around our necks and had to be careful not to bruise the fruits as we picked them. He also had many soft fruit bushes and I can remember the gooseberries with their whiskers on. He also kept rabbits, hens and pigeons so it was a really busy place. Granny Gregory was very Victorian. Born in 1880, she still wore a long black skirt on top of which was a 'good' apron, then a course apron, usually a piece of sacking to keep the other apron clean. Her hair went down to her waist and, each day, she would stand and brush it for ages as a way of keeping it clean, then roll it up into a bun. I don't think she ever washed her hair and when she had to go into hospital and they washed it, it was snow white, whereas I had only ever seen it a sort of iron grey.

I don't know what year their cottage was built. I believe it belonged to the Delves Broughton family at Dorfold Hall. When Grandad purchased it, mother told me that he walked from Coppenhall to Dorfold Hall with the cash in his pocket - £400 which was obviously a lot of money then. They never seemed to be short of cash, though. In fact I also believe that they would loan money to neighbours and no doubt they made a little profit from that enterprise. The cottage had two bedrooms; the second bedroom was accessed by a door from the first, but you had to step over a large beam to get in. When you stood by the window, your knees would be half way up the glass. There was no bathroom and no connection to the sewers. Downstairs, there was a parlour, living room and kitchen. The kitchen had been added to the property.

The parlour was never used even though the front door opened into it. I never knew of a time when the front door was actually opened, however, as you always entered from the back door. It was furnished with some very nice, but old fashioned pieces. The living room had a very nice chaise longue, covered in newspaper. On the side wall hung a long case clock with glass sides. This always had a glass paper weight placed inside with a picture of Abraham Lincoln encased in it. A kitchen table had a scrubbed top and of course the newspaper covering, then there were two kitchen chairs with wicker seating and a large leather chair with large lion heads carved on the arms. Strangely, this was never sat on, merely turned inwards and also covered in newspaper. A bamboo-legged table stood in the corner with the wireless on top. Heavy lace curtains hung from a thick brass pole with blackout roller blinds from the war serving as the draw curtains. The fire grate was a large black one with open fire and an oven and hob to one side. The 'new' kitchen had a concrete floor where, years later, Granny had a 'Baby Belling' electric cooker. The sink was a shallow brown one with a wooden drainer and in the corner was the built in coal-heated washing boiler.

My recollection of having tea with Granny was of having to speak only when spoken to. Tea always consisted of bread and jam. Granny had a real knack of being able to slice bread perfectly and almost paper thin. The butter was always applied first before cutting. Grandad Gregory was a very kind, gentle, learned man. I only knew him as an 'old person' as he was 69 when I was born. Having snow white hair and moustache to match, and short in stature, he was profoundly deaf - caused no doubt by his job as a riveter in the boiler shop at Crewe Works. He lost an eye in an accident at work there and I often remember this eye turning round the wrong way in his eye socket, obviously not fitting that well. You had to shout very loudly: 'Grandad, your eye has turned round'. With no more ado, he would take it out, turn it round, and put it back in while you watched.

I do recall the story of him going to just one football match at Crewe Alex. Apparently he threw his cap into the air and never saw it again. That was the end of going to football matches as he said he couldn't afford a new cap every time. He owned two very large beautiful tool boxes which housed the joinery tools of his father who was a carpenter on the barges in Winsford during the mid 1800s. These are still in the family, loved and adored by my eldest brother who still uses them.

Christmas was always an exciting time and it did not seem to matter that we didn't get much from Father Christmas because we never expected to. We received one main present and a few bits and bobs in our woolly sock. I always remember a tree, no electric lights, of course, but small candles in holders clipped to the end of the

150

branches. We used to make our own streamers. Chicken was always on the menu as this was expensive and a real treat.

Apart from holidaying at the farm, I was taken on holiday with friends, camping in North Wales. This was the first time that I climbed Snowdon when I was probably about 13. Days out were also had with our neighbours, the Lathams who had three boys who were my mates. We went off to Brown's Moss or Prees Heath aerodrome in their Bedford Dormobile for a day's adventure. I also holidayed with another friend whose parents had a chalet at Talacre. Their car was a Morris or Austin, the one with the spare tyre on the back and with a pull-down luggage carrier in front. My first ride in a car was a memorable one in a baby Austin owned by Sid Robinson from next door but one. Off we went along the country lanes, seemingly going fast. The trouble with this car was that the rear doors didn't shut properly. Over Minshull Canal bridge we went at great speed and laughter when, suddenly, the doors opened. Fortunately, Sid had put hook and Eye catches in place to stop them opening completely!

Holidays for all the family came about when I was around seven years of age. These were taken at Tyn-y-Morfa near to Gronant, North Wales. We hired the holiday home 'Abbey View' from the Quimbys, a local family who owned one of the local shops. It was a former railway carriage, the type that had little windows in the shaped roof. It had been fitted out really nicely, with two bedrooms sleeping three people and a central living/kitchen area. No water or mains toilet, but that didn't bother us. The lighting was by gas mantle, which also helped to keep you warm on a chilly summer's evening. One year, Dad has been on holiday for a few days and we were due to go away in the second week. A knock came on the front door; it was my father's foreman from the north shed.

'Stan, can you come in and drive the Queen's train on Saturday?' Well my heart sank; knowing how proud he was that he was being asked *again* to drive this special train. Dad said 'yes' immediately. Well I wasn't having any of that! I started pulling and poking at my father to get his attention. 'What's the matter, can't you see I'm talking?'

'But Dad,' I said. 'We go on holiday on Saturday.' Well, his face and that of his foreman dropped and, yes, I won and we went on holiday.

Shopping in those days was at the Co-op on the corner of Holland Street. What an experience. The money was placed in little containers sent flying on wires to the cash office. Sugar was weighed into blue strong paper bags, biscuits were bought loose, and butter, cheese etc were cut by a wire and weighed out. No self service, of course, and you were served over a counter by an assistant. We also had four shops on the end of our street in Underwood Lane, known as the 'top shops'. (Little did I know then that my husband, Barrie, would own three of them in later years). My elder sister, Jen, went dancing most weekends at the town hall. I used to love seeing her in her dance dresses. One week she came home from town after purchasing some glitter from Woolworths which you painted on your hair. Mother thought she would give this a try. She dusted it on and it was fine. Later in the day, however, she wet her hair and it promptly turned green and stayed like that for many days!

Mother didn't have a very happy life when we were small children. It was probably caused by post-natal depression which wasn't recognized or treated in those years. This resulted in her not going out of the house unless it was dark and then she would only venture to the front gate or take a walk around the block.

Crewe Carnival was a really big event back in my and my children's childhood. The procession took around two hours to get along West Street where we always watched it. I can see the hoards of people now walking up Underwood Lane in time for the procession to pass by. The big show tents were erected in the park for the local people to 'show' their products from their gardens; flowers, fruit or vegetables and homemade produce like jam and chutney. Grandad Gregory always had honey on show and mainly won. He also showed his home grown fruit and veg. This skill he passed on to my father. The apples especially had to be polished with newspaper until you could see your face in them. Carrots and parsnips had to be long and straight, onions as big as footballs. It was a sight to behold.

A LIFE OF CARING AND CURING

by Tripta Schur

I was born in Nairobi, Kenya, of Indian parents who were born in India and moved to Kenya after their marriage in the mid-1940s. My father had a family business and worked hard like a lot of Asians. My grandfather was Head Postmaster General at the Post Office in Nairobi. We did not have home delivery of letters but had an allocated post box at the General Post Office and we used to enjoy taking turns to open the box and see what mail was inside. My maternal uncle was Head Station Master in Jinja, Uganda, and we often spent school holidays with his family. He used to let us wave the flag at the station steam trains – we loved doing that!

We lived in an area of Nairobi where most residents were Indians, Punjabis, Gujratis and Sikhs. This helped our communication skills with different languages. I went to primary school locally, but after 11-plus exams I went to an English-speaking school – the Duchess of Gloucester where most of the teachers were Scottish and very strict. It was compulsory to speak English, even during playtime. I often got caught by prefects talking Hindi and was given detention (made to stand outside the head's office at playtime). We started school at 8 a.m. till 1 p.m. and afternoons were for games and sport three times a week. I played tennis and hockey. I never enjoyed swimming and still don't, although I have taken up canoeing and have made some effort in staying afloat.

As children, we spoke English as our common language, partly to improve and help my mother who did not learn English as a child. We played in each other's gardens and also in the streets and parks, simple games like rounders, marbles and wheel rolling with a stick. We shared many happy meals as there was no formality – a custom in Indian households that you provide the best for anyone who happens to call on you. I remember my father often coming home from office with a colleague without pre-warning mother. She was always delighted to share food with anyone.

153

After my 'A' level exams, I left for India to study medicine as an overseas student. There were no medical schools in Kenya, the first only started in 1970. Leaving home for the first time was very traumatic. I can still remember my mother sobbing when the ship set sail from Mombasa to Bombay. I was just 17 and she believed that she had lost me. I was met by my maternal uncle and aunt at the dock in Bombay, whom I had never met. They only had a small photograph to pick me out of nearly 500 other students.

After six days at sea among all students - a very memorable journey of my life - I was exposed to life in India. This was a shock to the system, something that, in retrospect I do relish. Five years in medical school was a great experience. The first day at the anatomy hall gave me nightmares, however. Never can one forget when you face bodies on long tables ready for dissection. I attended medical school in Jaipur, the largest city in the northern state of Rajasthan, where I made a lot of friends (I'm still in contact with some). One particular family, of the Professor of Anatomy, looked after me as their own. Sadly he and his wife have passed away, but their children are great friends. I visited a lot of my maternal relatives in Northern India, around Delhi at that time, too.

On returning to Kenya, I worked at a local hospital and also did a lot of community medicine in small villages. One clinic was run during the day in a shack which, by night, was used for social events – on occasion it was also used as a drinking den by some of the young men with their home brew. Some patients, especially small children, were brought in almost terminally ill with malaria, dehydration, or some other ailment by their parents who had walked for several miles to get there. They would often sit for hours before the clinic opened, just to be seen by a doctor. After a year of voluntary work, I decided to be independent and leave home for England.

My first job at Nottingham General Hospital in the casualty department was a completely new experience, especially hearing the choice language on Friday and Saturday nights! The next step was to move to Banbury as Senior House Officer. I met my future husband, Paul, who, too, was Senior House Officer. We married and moved to Plymouth where Paul completed his General Practitioner training and

154

I worked part time in family planning. We started having our own family (so I didn't practice what I preached!); I had two children, a son and a daughter. We moved to Crewe in 1979 and our third child, a daughter, was born in 1981 at Leighton hospital.

There is quite a bit of 'medicine' in the family. Our teacher son, Ben, is married to Anna, a GP, and they live in Plymouth with their two children. Our older daughter, Kauta, is a doctor at present working in New Zealand along with her husband. Our second daughter – Athene, married with a baby, is Senior Cardiac Nurse at the Royal Wolverhampton Hospital.

Having worked in General Practice at Wells Green Surgery for 21 years, I decided to take early retirement to pursue my hobbies and interests. Sewing and knitting have been one of my pastimes since childhood. Unknown to my mother, I remember knitting a small cardigan for my baby brother at the age of 10. I can also claim to have stitched a wedding dress for one of our daughters! Other hobbies include playing tennis and hill walking, especially long distance walks anywhere in the world. I have even done some trekking in the Himalayas at 14,000 feet in the snow. I also started Canadian canoeing on long stretches of rivers, especially in Scotland and I have also done Loch Ness to raise funds for the RNLI. I find gardening great fun and very therapeutic and I find time to read – especially thrillers. There is also bird watching and voluntary work for the RSPB and, of course, work at the clinic in the hills above Darjeeling where there is no medical care.

THE MAGIC OF MYFANWY

by Jean Scott

Memories, but how to choose? From a lifetime of over 70 years; many happy memories, yet some sad and painful. I think that I shall tell you of a particularly magical evening, in the summer when the air was soft and gentle and the light was beginning to fade. My brother and I were in our early teens. My father, an outdoor man, loved the open countryside, especially the Welsh mountains and valleys, a passion that he passed on to his children.

He had bought three bicycles, one for himself and one each for me and my brother. After some practice days out around Staffordshire, Cheshire and Derbyshire, he began to take us away for several days at a time around North and Mid Wales.

On one of these trips we had travelled up the coast from Mid Wales before turning inland towards home via Bala and Corwen and down through Llangollen. Keeping the river on our left we passed underneath the Pontcysyllte aqueduct and turned left into the village where we had booked a night's rest at the local youth hostel.

After our evening meal, we took a walk up through the village to explore. The long main street curved slightly uphill opening onto a square. A hall at the corner of the square showed lights through the high windows and one or two men were drifting in. We didn't stop to see what was going on as my father had heard the sound of a river. We saw a small humpbacked bridge on the right-hand side of the square and went to investigate.

The grass by the river side was short and soft. We climbed the low wall and sat on the grass listening to the sound of the water as it swished and bubbled along to disappear under the bridge. Suddenly, dad stopped talking. 'Listen,' he said, 'I can hear music.' I couldn't hear anything at first, then just faintly. 'It's a choir,' said dad. 'Let's go and see.'

We were soon over the wall, trying to keep up with father as he strode off towards the hall. There were no posters to advertise a concert and the doors were shut, but the wonderful sound of the choir drifted through the open windows.

It was a lovely gentle warm evening. We leaned on the wall and listened as the choir started a new refrain, a lovely haunting melody, the voices rising and falling to make the most beautiful sound I'd ever heard. They were singing in Welsh, of course, so I didn't understand the words, but one word was repeated several times throughout the song, *Myfanwy*, which has been a favourite song ever since, as also have Welsh male voice choirs. It is a sound like no other; magical music to stir the soul or to drift over you bringing calm and peace. This was the early days of the now-famous Fron Male Voice Choir.

Another notable memory is from the late 1980s when I was asked if I would paint a picture of HMS Endurance, the Royal Navy's Antarctic Survey ship otherwise known as 'The Red Plum' due to the fact she was painted red to show up against the snow and ice. I hunted through many magazines and books for information to work with. Not being able to find anything of use, I wrote to the ship's captain. A couple of months later, a large packet arrived. It was from Captain Nick Barker, captain of Endurance. The package contained a number of beautiful photos of the ship from all angles, and also photos of the new ship which was being prepared to replace it. There were also stunning photos of the Antarctic landscape and a lovely brochure with all the details I needed.

I set to work planning my picture. I sent off sketches to the ship for approval and to make sure I had everything right. During this period the old ship was retired and the new ship came into service with her captain Bob Turner who would become my new contact. I decided to put both ships into the painting and set to work on the canvas. As with any oil painting and detailed work it was a lengthy process. Eventually finished, both captains requested a viewing and my husband and I went to visit Nick Barker in North Shields. He was delighted with the result and I promised that he could have one of the first prints.

We also travelled to Plymouth when the new ship arrived following Bob Turner's invitation to lunch on board the ship with him. He was delighted with the picture and managed to get my

157

husband to part with it, as it had been intended for him. The painting was hung in the Trophy Gallery on board the ship and has been photographed with many dignitaries who have visited the vessel.

Following the success of the Endurance painting, I have painted a series of Royal Naval ships associated with the North West, and so followed, HMS Ambuscade for Crewe sailing off South Georgia, HMS Liverpool sailing up the River Mersey and HMS Broadsword for Chester, taking part in sea trials off the south coast. The final one in the chain, the latest nuclear submarine HMS Vanguard, built in Barrow-in-Furness.

The latter subject also involved lunch with the captain and a guided tour of the vessel - all after a tight-security screening. I was also asked to sign the visitor's book and was quite honoured to see that the only other signature was that of ...Princess Diana.

NOT MUCH 'STUFF' BUT STILL HAPPY

by Helen Slattery

I was born at home in Park Drive, Wistaston. I have four or five memories of the environment, not the actual house. One of which is when several very small children got into Dad's car and my older brother released the handbrake. The landlord's garage door took a bit of a knock! We moved to Nantwich when I was about five to another rented house on Wellington Road. This house had no central heating, no hot water upstairs, etc. I can remember gas lights. Mum's sole mod-con was a gas stove. Washing was done in the 'copper' (with a fire to heat the water), rinsed in the sink and passed through a large mangle. It was then hung outside to dry.

Sometimes the washing line broke and Mum had to start again if the lawn was muddy. Shopping was done daily as we had no fridge to keep food cold. Until we were old enough to help with the cleaning, our main chore was going to the shops for 'forgotten' items. My younger brother remembers us being sent to Stennett and Afford for salt. At the counter we were asked what sort of salt? We had no idea and so were sent home with a small bag of cooking salt. Mum was 'salting' runner beans (to preserve them). She was not happy with the salt we brought and sent us back for a block of salt. This was so bulky that even two small children had difficulty bringing it home.

Coal fires did not keep us particularly warm, even downstairs. They did mean, however, that we had the excitement of the chimney sweep once or twice a year and the soot came in very handy for the garden. But I can't remember for what it was considered useful. Dad had an allotment across the road. He grew some vegetables but mostly fruit. Mum made jam and bottled fruit.

My primary school was Wayside School in Hospital Street. This was a very small school of three classes. The fees must have been low as my parents were far from rich and I had two brothers. My friends included the daughter of a local chemist and the daughter of a farm manager. Occasionally I visited the farm at Wardle. I went on the bus with a label in my coat to tell the conductor where to put me off. We must have lived in a very safe environment as we walked unaccompanied to school and to Brownies. I remember meeting my cousin off the Stoke bus.

One day, I had been given a thermos of water to top up the flower vases on the altar of St Mary's church. We couldn't get the top off the thermos flask and nor could a man we approached outside the church. So we had to do what my mother wanted to avoid - carry the heavy vases to the tap in the porch room. Needless to say, I knocked over a vase when replacing it on the altar. We were so horrified that we took to our heels and fled home in panic.

Family holidays were almost always self-catering in Wales and I mean self-catering, apart from ice cream, I don't think we ever ate out. Our luggage went ahead by rail. The family of five plus the dog followed in the car. Not a seatbelt in sight. I tended to suffer from car sickness and lay down on the back seat with my poor brothers perched on the edge. One time we went to Dorset and accidentally left the dog tied up at the car-park - until someone remembered him!

We had a happy childhood although by modern standards we had the minimum of 'stuff'. Most other people seemed to be in the same boat. We wore hand-me downs and hand knitted or sewn garments. Make-do and mend was the order of the day. I think this was a time of austerity and Dad's job was not well-paid. He was a school dentist and travelled from village school to village school. We didn't have a television until I was about 13 - after the Queen's Coronation which we watched on our Stoke cousin's set – in black and white, of course. I do remember seeing a film (in colour) of the Coronation at the cinema. We had a radio but weren't encouraged to make free with it. I was a big reader and frequented Nantwich library. The books tended to date to my mother's era which was fine with me as they were the books we had at home.

Christmas was a time for home-made paper chains and Dad's socks used as Christmas stockings. As I recall, we had one present, then the stocking which contained the nuts and tangerines. We never had a turkey. Once or twice we had a goose. Usually it was a chicken and that was the only time we had chicken all year. I was about 11

160

before I realised chicken had white meat! I don't know why chicken was so expensive, no battery hens, I suppose. Bonfire Night was also a time for a party. Families did their own thing or combined their efforts. The bonfire was an essential part. Health and Safety had not been heard of. Some children made a guy and put it in a soapbox cart and begged for 'pennies for the guy'. There was no such thing as Trick or Treat at Halloween.

OVER-BOILED CABBAGE – AGAIN!

by Brenda Smethurst

I was born in July 1949 in Manchester at Park Hospital where the NHS had been launched exactly a year earlier by Aneurin Bevan, and which has now, as Trafford General, sadly lost its A&E facility. We lived in a quiet crescent with a grass croft where all the local kids played with a freedom that is alien to the kids of today. Out of the 40 or so houses in our crescent, only a couple had a car during the 1950s, so we walked everywhere or used public transport. It was still safe to cycle anywhere and, as older kids, we used to ride a dozen miles or more, taking a picnic with us as long as we had a friend to go with.

Our house was a semi-detached in Davyhulme, about six miles from the city centre where my Dad worked as a textile designer for a large cotton firm, He was always worried about redundancy when other dads seemed to be secure in their various employments, and money was always tight in our house. We did manage one week's holiday a year, taken at the same boarding house in Blackpool, which we loved. When I was 12, Mum eventually returned to work part-time as a secretary and Dad later changed jobs to become a wallpaper designer for Crown when he was 52, which is when we got our first car – I was 20 and at Library School.

Dad had been in the army for six years during WW2 and frequently old pals would come round in the evening to reminisce (Dad was never one for going down the pub). As far as I recall, Mum was usually in the kitchen most evenings baking endless cakes, puddings and pies for our family. .

Food was very boring in this era; always meat and two veg for main meals, with over-boiled cabbage served up more often than not. We all hated being called in for meals as it interfered with our play, and we were never allowed to have the TV on while we ate, except (for some unknown reason) on a Saturday teatime. Dad would only ever let us watch BBC as he considered ITV to be a corrupting influence with inferior programmes. (I never saw Coronation Street, for instance, until I was married and living down south!).

We didn't have a TV until 1954, so we went to my uncle's to watch the Coronation in 1953. I don't remember much about it except that I wore red, white and blue socks and hair ribbons. A large Union Jack was flown from an upstairs' window in our house. My brother was born a month later, and after 10 day's stay in hospital (the norm in those days), Mum brought him home on my fourth birthday and announced he was my 'birthday present'. I was most put out as I'd set my heart on having a sister, and I never fully recovered from my disappointment! We fought like cat and dog throughout our childhood.

Very occasionally, before I started school, I would spend the weekend, accompanied by my older cousin, at my grandparent's house a few miles away. I always enjoyed this event, the highlight being a Mars bar bought by our Nan which had to be carefully broken in half and shared. We were not allowed to touch any of the highly-polished surfaces in our grandparent's home, nor allowed to play their piano which we longed to do even though we had one in our own house. But the biggest temptation was to visit their air-raid shelter in the back garden, which was a source of constant fascination to us. For some reason we were never allowed to go near it, and the same applied to our neighbours' shelters. To this day I cannot understand their reluctance to show us inside, which would have no doubt quenched our curiosity once and for all.

Our milk and bread was delivered daily by horse and cart and our crescent's gas lamps were regularly maintained by a chap who used to give us the empty gas mantel boxes. We used these to house our 'stable' of caterpillars which we used to 'race'. In spring, we would go down to the local brook to collect frog spawn near the Manchester Ship Canal where we used to marvel at the ocean liners 'sailing' through the fields. All the Crescent kids played out after tea even on winter evenings and especially when it was icy. We made the most terrific slides, perfecting them until they shone like the moon - until one poor old lady fell and hurt herself. We were most put out that we had to destroy that particular slide. We climbed trees, made dens, roller-skated, played cricket and football (girls and boys), as well as

163

the usual skipping, whip and top, hula-hooping and playing games such as 'What time is it Mr. Wolf' and 'Grandmother's footsteps'. We also had a 'truck' made by our Dad from an old pram chassis, which seemed to ensure we had permanently-bruised shins. We got up to the usual naughty tricks when in a gang, and once organized a flower show by picking all the best flowers from the neighbours' gardens and arranging them in a tasteful display on our croft for all to admire. Of course, there was an almighty row over that and we never dared do it again. We regularly played 'White Rabbit' when it was dark; someone (usually the youngest child) was sent to knock on a neighbour's door, and then we all legged it, hiding when the door was opened.

When I started school aged five, the nearest school was already full, due to the baby boomers, so I had to attend one about three miles away, which entailed a bus journey. On my first day, every child in my class (except me) was left sobbing when their mothers left them to go home - none of us had been separated from our mums before. During my whole school career, I only cried once. This was in my first year at school when my penny bus fare was stolen from my purse in the cloakroom and I didn't know how I would get home. The teacher lent me a penny but said I must be sure to bring it back the following day. I burst into tears because I couldn't comprehend just how I was supposed to hand that penny to the bus conductor, yet return it the next day!

Another time, again in my first year, I had bad toothache in the morning and told my teacher who said there was nothing that could be done, and that I must wait until home time at 3.30 p.m. I decided to walk home on my own at dinnertime, which took an hour or so. Mum took me to the local dentist who extracted the tooth, and when we arrived back home the headmistress was waiting in her car (a Jowett Javelin I recall, as I knew all the makes of cars at five years old), to take me back to school. She was fine about my escapade, but my teacher was very angry with me. I was only ever smacked once at school - when I was seven - for being the slowest in needlework. I was most affronted by this, thinking it was extremely unfair. Someone had to be last.

Looking back to the 1950s, I'm surprised how, on the one hand, children were expected to be quite mature in many ways, such as looking after younger siblings all day, or running endless errands to the local shops or beyond at a very young age, and being expected to come home with the goods and the right change. Yet, on the other hand, adults were loathe to give us any information deemed unsuitable, such as why a grandparent was going into hospital, even for a minor operation, so that such an incident grew in immensity in our imagination.

I remember going into the dining room during one family party and overhearing the adults talking about George Formby. I must have been around seven or eight years old and as soon as they saw me I was shooed out of the room and the door was firmly shut in my face. Years later I discovered that he'd left his wife for someone else, yet something so trite was considered entirely unsuitable for my ears. How times have changed!

SUCH A THRILL TO GO TO RHYL

by Neil Smith

I was born in Bedford in 1940 and don't remember much about the war, although I was told that, during air raids, I was put in a basket under the stairs. I was the youngest of five brothers. I believe my parents thought I was the last chance of having a girl – sorry to disappoint them. On VE day in May 1945, we received special vouchers to take part in entertainments in the town so we had an exciting trip on the local boating lake. In that year I went on my very first holiday to Rhyl in North Wales. My mother wrote a poem about it: *This summer we're going to Rhyl, O won't it be such a thrill!* and there was a line about *having bananas again with their shiny yellow coats.* There was rationing, of course, which didn't completely end until the early Fifties and we had to 'make do and mend'. I was always disappointed that railway stations had machines for chocolate bars which couldn't be worked. I do remember regularly going to our sweet shop with a coupon to get a quarter pound of fruit sweets.

My father was a popular optician and worked very hard with his business – in fact he didn't retire until he was 75. My mother helped, too, and cycled down to the shop every afternoon. She did all the accounts and paperwork. Most days they also brought papers home and did more work in the evening. Of course, there weren't many cars in those days and everyone walked or cycled. Dad was cycling to work one day and paused at the 'Stop' sign at the bottom of our road. He'd no sooner set off again when he was immediately challenged by a police sergeant who said Dad had failed to put his foot on the ground! It seems ludicrous compared to nowadays when whole families ride on the pavement and go without lights, completely oblivious to the Highway Code – and unchallenged by any policeman.

We had a large end-terraced house with four bedrooms and another in the attic. We even had a bathroom although we continued to use chamber pots until the early 1950s. The back garden was only small, but we were fortunate to live opposite a large park in which I spent many happy hours. One of my expeditions there was to catch Great Crested Newts from a small pond. I'd tie a worm to a short length of string then wait a short while. Once a newt got its mouth on a worm it wouldn't let go so they were quite easy to catch. I'd put them in a jam jar and keep them at home in a goldfish bowl – our cat was fascinated watching them, but he never tried to catch them.

We had four downstairs rooms in the house; the scullery for all the washing and cooking, the kitchen with a large round table where we usually sat for meals, the dining room was used for special occasions and for Dad's business work in the evening. The drawing room had comfortable arm chairs and a piano and tended to be used on Sundays and for visitors. Kitchen heating was by coke boiler while the dining and drawing rooms had open fires. Like most houses of the time, there was no heating upstairs and we relied on old stone water bottles to keep us warm in winter. After a cold night, it was not unusual to wake up to find ice on the inside of the windows.

I sometimes helped mother with washing on Mondays and she started using the new-fangled Twin Tub machine, but the clothes still needed to go through the old mangle. All the boys and Dad wore white shirts with detachable collars which had to be starched. There were clean collars every one or two days, but shirts and underwear had to last for a week. I'm not sure what we smelt like on a Saturday morning and when you consider we didn't use deodorant then! I can't remember any girls or friends complaining though.

My Dad was a Baptist preacher for over 60 years and regularly cycled to country villages on Sundays to take services in Methodist and Congregational churches as well as Baptist. So I had a fairly strict upbringing. On Sundays we went to church three times including the Sunday school in the afternoon. There was the annual Sunday School Anniversary where we were put on a platform at the front of the church to sing special hymns and children were given a prize book for regular attendance. There was also an annual outing by coach to seaside places like Clacton on the East Coast.

When I was 10 or 11 my regular hobby was train spotting and I used to spend many hours by the line-side or on stations collecting engine numbers. With a friend, I travelled by train to many towns and cities all over the country. I remember that on several occasions we went from Bedford to London (50 miles) on the 6.30a.m. train which had a special workman's cheap ticket at only three shillings and sixpence (17 ½ p). With the help of a special guide book we then proceeded to travel by underground train or bus to many of the locomotive depots. Trying to avoid being seen by the foreman, we went up and down the rows of steam engines collecting the numbers. There were many hazards – not only huge engines moving around but smoke, steam, water, oil and hot cinders. Looking back, this was all quite dangerous and parents today would have a fit. To us, the sight, sounds and smell of locomotives made it a great adventure. When I got home at the end of the day, I would call at the chip shop for a large threepenny bag of chips to be devoured with a poached egg when I got home.

My brothers had all been to a small primary school, expertly run by two elderly ladies. When my turn came, they had retired and so my parents sent me to a local teacher training school. Unfortunately the school failed to make much of an impression me. My parents really wanted me to get me into the grammar school (as all my brothers had done) but my standard was far too low. So they sent me to a small private preparatory school which was run by a retired teacher. He was assisted by two ex-army assistant masters, a Colonel Dabson and Major McVittie. I remember doing a maths lesson where some of the sums were quite difficult. 'Blow this,' I thought, 'I can't be bothered.' So I just put random numbers in the answer. Major McVittie was not amused – he put me over his knee and walloped my behind. I never did it again!

With their help and encouragement I did manage to scrape into the grammar school – which was one of the minor public schools. When I arrived at Bedford Modern School in 1950 there were approx. 950 boys (there was also a similar school for girls). There were monitors (prefects) who were allowed to cane their underlings for any misdemeanour and quite often boys received a savage beating. This was abolished shortly after I arrived but some masters continued to cane regularly. I suffered twice. First when a boy hit me in the face with a paper pellet and I threw it back at him. Unfortunately this was spotted by the master and I was caned while the other boy got off. The second time was when I failed to do my chemistry homework (called prep). I have to say though that these events and the school ethos had an entirely beneficial effect on me, so I completely accept the old Bible adage 'spare the rod and spoil the child.' Many may disagree, but my view is that 'proper' discipline by parents and schools would prevent many of the evils around us today.

Everything in school was done to a regular timetable including attendance on Saturday mornings. We felt proud to belong to a school established in the era of Elizabeth I. In the evenings they had a system called 'lockup' which ruled that no boy should be outside their house after 6.30pm in winter and 8.30pm in summer. This was meant to ensure that children stayed in to do their homework properly which could take from two to four hours a night. Sport took place every Wednesday and Saturday afternoon and most boys were expected to take part. I was never very good, but always aspired to do better. I managed to get in the house second cricket and rugby teams. I also did a little rowing in an annual event called 'house fours' – very hard work even for 400 yards if you didn't do it regularly. Every spring term there was the annual 'Steeplechase' where every boy was expected to run four to five miles across fields and up hills. Every boy was expected to learn to swim in the school's swimming bath and until you could swim your 'pass' of two lengths (66 yards), you were made to wear a white button on your cap – some ignominy! Most of us also joined the school army cadet force where strict discipline ruled again. We all took our marching, map reading and rifle training very seriously. Competitions were held with other schools to find those who were the smartest at drilling and band playing. In the summer we went away to a regular army camp in Thetford, Norfolk or Pirbright, Surrey and had mock battle in cross country exercises. Later I had the chance to join the RAF section and had the thrill of flying for the first time in a somewhat ancient aircraft (an ex-wartime Avro Anson).

I did struggle through school and, without my mother's brilliant help with English and Maths, I might have failed miserably. Standards were higher then but in my final year I managed to pass five GCEs which I thought was not bad after such a poor start.

All my brothers had done National Service but it came to an end in 1958, so I missed it by about six months. It might have done me some good and given me more confidence as I was rather shy – especially with girls!

My elder brother had a good job as an operating manager with British Rail and I always aspired to follow him. Most boys got jobs immediately on leaving school as there wasn't much unemployment in the late 50s. So I applied and got a job on the railway as a junior booking clerk at Harlington - a country station on the main line south of Bedford. I received the grand salary of £208 per annum which was paid fortnightly. This was still in the steam era of course. On my first day I started training with the Station Master who engulfed me with clouds of cigarette smoke from his woodbines! Instruction was also given by Ernie Hassall, the goods clerk, who was the last clerk on the former Midland Railway to be issued with a uniform (pre 1923). We covered many things besides tickets. Parcels were received or despatched by almost every passenger train. Large amounts of parcels from Littlewoods and other mail order companies had to be recorded and delivered by BR lorry. We also sent out quantities of spring bulbs in bags all over the country. London's rubbish was received in train loads to a special siding for disposal and a nearby cement works sent out many wagons to Birmingham and London.

After gaining more experience at two other stations, I was promoted to a position at Euston headquarters in 1960 which meant an early start and commuting 50 miles every day from Bedford to London. It was a very interesting job involving many aspects of railway operation between Euston and a point south of Rugby. Timekeeping of trains was monitored very closely and delays of even a few minutes were investigated and reports called for from everyone concerned. Instructions were sent out not only by letter and phone but in many cases by internal telegrams which used special codewords to save space.

After studying lots of rules and regulations, I was very lucky to be appointed Station Master (Temporary) at Castle Ashby & Earls Barton – a country station between Northampton and Wellingborough in Northamptonshire. At the age of 21, I believe I was one of the youngest in the country at that time. It was a fairly quiet station with about 14 passenger and one pick-up goods train each day. I was responsible for supervising station staff, two signal boxes and three level crossings. I also had to do all passenger, parcels and goods accounts and weekly wage and income tax calculations. Livestock such as cattle and sheep were received or sent out from the goods yard. The Station Master then was considered to be part of the community and I was also expected to visit local firms to canvass for business. I travelled by motor bike every day from Bedford eventually buying my first car, a 1948 Ford Anglia for the princely sum of £40. In this I did a 40 mile round trip every day clocking up 20,000 miles in 12 months.

A year later I was back at the Euston HQ and asked to take on a post as Relief Station Master at Bletchley, Bucks. In this new job I could be called to take charge of any station or marshalling yard between Euston and Wolverton (about 70 miles). Most stations were different and I had to find out the routines and peculiarities for myself and at the same time supervise 50-150 staff. When the Queen was travelling by Royal Train one night, I was required to attend a country station at 1am in the morning to check everything was safe. At some of the larger depots, payment of wages was a major operation as several hundred staff would all be paid in cash. At some places, we even had a police escort. During the Beeching era in the 1960s, many smaller stations and country lines closed and lots of staff were made redundant. For the following 30 years there were major changes in the management and organisational structure almost every year – nothing stayed the same for long.

THE DAY THE KING DIED

by Trevor Thomas

This is by no means my earliest memory, but it is certainly the earliest that I can relate to a specific date, 6 February 1952. A few days before my seventh birthday, I was walking the mile or so home from school for lunch (then pronounced 'dinner'). Nearing home, I reduced my pace in order to stay several yards behind three slow-moving boys from the local senior school, being worried that they might 'get' me if I attempted to overtake them. I then overheard one of them quip: 'Who's going to be King now - Winston Churchill!' at which they all laughed. Arriving home, I asked my mother: 'Is the King dead?' My mother said she thought not, then turned on the radio (pronounced 'wireless'). Instead of the usual joviality of the likes of Wilfred Pickles or Worker's Playtime, the Light Programme was playing a mournful selection of slow and solemn music. My mother was immediately aware of the implication, and she shed a few tears. But my concerns had moved on. 'What's for dinner?' I enquired.

BLIGHTY AND FAR BEYOND

by Doreen Thorpe

I was born on 12th June 1930 in a railway-owned two-up two-down cottage in Pendlebury near Manchester. Father was a Welshman who had migrated from Anglesey. I had two brothers, Harry, aged 10, and Norman, aged nearly nine. Sadly, Norman was killed when knocked down by a lorry when I was just four months old. When I was three years old, I started in the nursery class of the local infants' school. I can remember little semi-circular chairs being suspended from the roof beams on long ropes. As I progressed through the school, we had to march into our classrooms each morning with the headmistress, Miss Lancaster, playing *The Keel Row* on the piano. I also remember that once a week we had to swallow Beecham's powder which was wrapped in individual paper wrappings.

When the First World War started in 1914, Dad joined the army and in 1915, when the First Battalion of the Welsh Guards was formed, he was invited to join the new regiment because of his Welsh connections. He was very proud of this and fought with them until the end of the war when they marched to Cologne as part of the occupying army and he was demobbed in 1919. He was not wounded at all, but was gassed which affected his breathing until his death in 1941 in a railway accident during the blackout. I don't know when he met my mother but they were married in Salford on 1st December 1917 when he was on leave. I know very little of my mother's early life, she seemed very unwilling to talk about it, but both their fathers had died by the time they were married.

My brother, Harry, badly wanted to join the Welsh Guards. Dad put him off by telling him all the difficulties of an army life. So he joined the Territorial Army instead when, at least, he could have a taste of it. At the outbreak of war, Harry was, therefore, one of the first men to be called up. He was serving in the Orkney Isles when Dad died and was spared serving overseas. That was because I had already been evacuated to Australia and if Harry had been posted abroad, Mum would have been left on her own - something the forces tried to avoid.

During the war nearly 3,000 children between the ages of five and 15 out of more than 200,000 applicants were sent abroad, mainly to Australia, Canada, South Africa and New Zealand. I was one of 477 children who went on a Polish ship, *MS Batori,* to Australia together with about 500 soldiers. We left Liverpool in early August 1940 arriving in Sydney 10 weeks later after an adventurous voyage, calling at Cape Town, Bombay and Singapore. We made very good friends of the soldiers who were on their way to Singapore and I am sure that most of them would have died or been taken prisoner by the Japanese when they invaded a few months later. While we were on our journey we heard that the ship, *City of Benares,* had been torpedoed by a German U-boat while on its way to Canada and that 260 lives had been lost, including 77 of the 90 child evacuees. As a result of this disaster the whole scheme of relocating children abroad was cancelled, but those of us already on our journey had to continue on our way.

I spent the rest of the war years in a beautiful town called Toowoomba situated on the Great Dividing Range about 100 miles inland from Brisbane in Queensland. If evacuees had relatives in Australia they were forced to live with them, which did not always go down very well. But those of us who had no one there lived with volunteers. I stayed with a couple who were both English-born and their two children, John about 15 months older than me and Jeannine, three years younger. They had another daughter while I was with them and another soon after I left to come home. I found it a bit difficult living with other children as I was used to being on my own. 'Auntie Joyce' Lindley was lovely but 'Uncle Charlie' was extremely strict and we were all somewhat afraid of him. He was 6ft 6ins tall and weighed 22 stone so we just had to do as we were told! Apart from that, I had a wonderful time and made good friends. I was very reluctant to come back to England at the end of the war and it was not possible for parents to go out there to join their children for another three years while the returning armed forces were resettled. I still keep in touch with John Lindley and also one of my school friends.

174

I came home at the end of 1945 - a shorter four week voyage through the Suez Canal - and immediately found it all so strange and difficult to settle. I was 15 and could have gone back to school but I knew from past experience that the education system was very different from that in Australia. I was also aware that my mother would find it difficult to cope as she now had to go to work and would not be able to afford to keep me as well. So I decided to start work,

My first job was as a messenger in the offices of the Exide Battery Co, later known as Chloride. The company employed about 2,000 people and I made lots of friends, including boyfriends. One special boy, Harry Smith, was great fun. He was in the army cadets as he badly wanted to join up and eventually fought in the Far East winning a medal. I remember seeing him on the news one day going to Buckingham Palace with Bill Speakman, an Altrincham boy, who had won the Victoria Cross.

When I was about 18, home life changed. My mother saw an advert in the local paper asking for sleeping accommodation for some of the resident doctors at the Royal Manchester Children's Hospital which was only about five minutes' walk from our house. We had one spare room available so she applied and from then on we had a succession of young men and women changing every six months. Every so often Mum would go over to see the Hospital Secretary to check that the arrangement was successful and as a result of this I was taken on in the medical records department. Eventually, my mother ended the arrangement and in 1954 a young man arrived seeking full time board and accommodation. His name was Stewart Thorpe. He worked at the Manchester Chloride Factory in the laboratory. Early in 1959 he took his final exams and as soon as this was done he felt free enough for us to become engaged, followed by our wedding in Matlock on 31st October, 1959. Sadly my mother had died in the previous May, but she had lived long enough to see me happily engaged. There followed nearly 50 years of happy and eventful married life.

175

PAST AND PRESENT – IN A FLASH

by Christopher Walsh

My tale is simple. It is about the way our senses connect our childhood with our present.

As a boy in the 1950s, my father would often take me to the Barton Swing Aqueduct over the Manchester Ship Canal. This was a place of boats, and grime, and smells and adventure that those who see beauty in industry, factories, and power stations, can understand best. For my father, a wistful man, it was the ships on the wide canal that held his attention.

For me, it was the coal-laden barges, en route to Barton Power Station, on the older, more compelling Bridgewater Canal that captured my imagination. The dank smell of coal-dust that swept up in the dirty wind from the magnificent wide barges into the tarry atmosphere of this industrial vista was matched only by the pungency of the grease that oiled the metalwork of the aqueduct. I was hooked. Not hooked by the same passions that arose within the silent fishermen that trawled the murky depths of the brown-grey Bridgewater for fish that, probably, were never there. Not drawn to the story of our British canals by books or lectures. No, it was through my senses, for I can still taste, smell, hear and feel the joy of what has been my lifelong passion.

I love our British waterways even now. I will walk their banks until the day I die. I write articles about them, and enthuse through presentations about their watery magnificence. The tang of rain-lashed grease is still in my nostrils. You? Yes you can raise those nostrils to a smell that remains with you even to this day. It may be less harsh than mine; bread, a puddle of water on a pram cover, a grandmother's sofa so distinctive it lingers so special, a sound or a mother's fingertips through your hair?

In this way your past is in your present. Wonderful, isn't it?

DOWN ON THE FARM

by Bob Welch

My story, but obviously not my memories, starts from when I was born in 1946. That was in a small village on the Essex/Hertfordshire border where my father was a farmer and my mother a farmer's wife. My father was from a farming family that went back to the mid-17th Century. Not surprisingly, my earliest memories were about farms and farming. By the time I was born, my father had progressed beyond horses to tractors, although the machines of those days bore no resemblance to today's models. By comparison, they were very rudimentary, open to all weathers, of limited power and sophistication but still of great fascination to a small boy. My most vivid recollections of this time are of the 'house cow' which, to a toddler, seemed huge and also of my father in the kitchen making butter! I don't think this event lasted much after the late 1940s as another recollection is of the weekly delivery of groceries from a shop in the local town. In fact I remember all sorts of things were delivered, milk, meat, bread and paraffin to mention just a few.

Although the farm was small by modern standards, it was of a sufficient size to employ two or three full time workers plus casual workers at busy times like the cereal harvest or for picking potatoes. In the early 1950s, the corn was cut by a binder and the sheaves carted in to make large stacks. These were subsequently thrashed by contractors who arrived at the farm for the job, the machinery being powered by steam engines which later gave way to diesel-powered tractors. I remember my father getting his first combine harvester, a Massey Harris - the days of the thrashing machine were finished. Similarly, the steam ploughing machines soon gave way to tractors. School holidays were spent back on the farm where driving a tractor was great fun. In these days of limited regulation I drove tractors from the age of about 10 and on the road at 12, illegal even then.

I suppose at the age of five I went to school, a small private school in Bishops Stortford, which was situated quite close to the

177

main London to Cambridge/ Kings Lynn railway line. Everyday we would watch an assortment of passenger and freight steam trains travelling up and down the line. I have interest in steam trains to this day. I suppose we must have learnt something, but recollections of the lessons are scanty. I do remember that school had no catering facilities because we used to go out to a local café for our lunches. The food was probably okay although I have hated custard to this day! Later, when we were older, seven or eight, a few of us would walk through the town to a different café and back completely unaccompanied. Holidays in the 1950s were spent at the seaside, usually the south coast or Devon or Cornwall. I remember going to the latter on a huge green steam train from Waterloo Station - what fun. I also remember swimming in the North Sea, so cold. When we went on holiday by car, my father would drive right through London if the route demanded it, no traffic problems or congestion charges in those days.

All this came to an end when, at the age of 10, I went to boarding school, a shock to the system at first, but one soon got used to it and there I remained for the next seven years. On occasions we would return to school by train, great fun and with all our trunks and other possessions we must have looked like something out of a *Harry Potter* film set. These schooldays were generally very enjoyable although this was still in the era of corporal punishment and 'fagging'. There didn't seem to be too much pressure to learn, but I passed all the necessary exams along the way to university.

The mid-Sixties saw me off to university to study agriculture thanks to a local authority grant. Based on parental income, for many students it meant no tuition fees in those days. A number of my friends who I met at university received the full grant and so effectively paid nothing for their tertiary education. Needless to say there was never enough money for us students! I might note in passing that, at the time I was at university, the town of Reading was one of the last in the UK to still have trolley buses, and a very good mode of transport they seemed to be. I remember in the early/mid 60s I could buy petrol at 4/10d a gallon and beer at 1/6d a pint - and there was no breathalyser either!

After university the world of work beckoned. There was little difficulty in finding a job in those days. Like for everybody, the world of work showed changes over the years. A few that come to mind are; demonstrating to a senior manager the efficacy of the purchase of an electronic calculator for office use. Well it was going to cost about £80 in 1972. Then the introduction of mobile phones (the first one I was given had a battery the size of about four bricks), and more latterly, of course, the introduction of computers.

FROM SLOW POST TO WI-FI

by Trish Welch

I grew up in the 1950s in a village south of Warrington. To get into town, we had to get a bus which went across the Manchester Ship Canal where there were several ships a day going up and down. In fact, one of my favourite bicycle rides was to Latchford Locks where we used to watch these huge ships, controlled by tugs, going into the small locks. Having crossed the canal, we then had to cross the level crossing railway and the 'new' bridge across the Mersey. The journey to the town's bus station, then the walk to one of the railway stations (Bank Quay for North-South) or (Central for East-West), took quite some time, so you always had to set off early and try to catch the bus in good time. In later days a bridge was built over the railway and fewer ships appeared.

In the 1960s I went to the grammar school at Lymm, which involved a seven-mile trip on the school bus which we caught from the middle of our village. Queuing could sometimes be a noisy affair as the stop was by the police station and the air-raid siren sometimes went off to alert the local fire brigade reserve officers of an emergency. These reserve firemen all lived in the one street and I remember watching them leaving their houses, rushing along and trying to climb into their uniforms at the same time.

I recall the bad winter in 1963 when the snow came down heavily and we ended up having to walk home from school because the buses couldn't reach us. We didn't have a landline then nor did any of my friends - so our parents had no idea of what was happening. It was after this, and after my grandmother was ill, that my parents applied for a telephone. They had to wait six months for it and then it was a shared line with our neighbours.

It was about this time that one of my uncles and his family became £10 'Poms' and went to Australia. Their voyage took six weeks. Letters to them generally went by boat, too, so communications were very slow. To call by phone was very expensive and had to be booked, so this was only done at Christmas.

In 2012, we were fortunate enough to visit Australia and we arrived at our hotel in Brisbane 24 hours after leaving home – what a contrast! We visited a second cousin, on my mother's side, whom we had found via the internet. We also discovered two other second cousins living nearby to us, and we were able to contact everyone at the same time via Skype; amazing! While in Australia, we visited the granddaughter and family of my uncle who had emigrated. We had lost touch with the family after both my father and my uncle died and my mother and aunt both became ill. But a letter from my cousin's daughter re-established contact and we were soon able to get in touch, exchanging messages and photographs at the touch of a button on the internet. Such progress when you compare it to bygone times.

MUSING THE MIND'S EYE

by Allan Whatley

I sit or lie down, take off my glasses and cover my eyes with my left hand. Darkness: I think of an incident of long ago. This is not preserved on any photograph whereby I would remember it easily and, yet, instantly I am able to 'see' the event. I ask myself if they are memories because each one was a surprise and thus unique?

We lived in a semi-detached house. Between one pair and the next there was a small brick building, some feet away from the house. It had two coalhouses and two toilets, back to back. Although built in 1919 the toilet, no longer down the garden path to the 'privy', was still outside the house. It was crudely ventilated by a three-inch gap above and below the door which made it bitterly cold most of the year. Mum used to put a candle-nightlight in there to 'take the chill off'. I remember hearing a man's voice when I was in the toilet. I realised it came from the Reverend Keys in his toilet. He was practising his sermon!

I was about six in 1919 when one of my mother's friends called. She had her little daughter of three or four with her. We two played in the garden. Suddenly the little girl lifted her frock and squatted. I was amazed! I soon noticed the difference between girls and boys and couldn't wait to run indoors and tell my mother.

One very hot summer, there was a fire on the moors, north of the boundary of Bournemouth. In the 1920s, we used to go to a small two-room cottage with a thatched roof owned by the Hulls, who were family friends. My father feared the blaze would reach us. The sheet of flame leapt high into the air and the noise of the crackling wood was terrific. Fortunately the fire service came and dealt with it. The Hulls owned a grocery business in Bournemouth and this cottage was their retreat. Emmie Hull lived past her 100th year. The moor has been built over now and small roads are named after them. We went to their house in Bournemouth on an occasion or two. I have two strong memories of those visits; I was allowed to 'play' the pianola

182

for a short while and I also discovered the National Geographic Magazine there – what a treasure.

Then there was the incident of the winter of about 1922 when I was nine. This was in Boscombe where my Dad ran one of the first wholefood shops. One of the first breakfast cereals was called 'Force'. It featured Sunny Jim: 'Force is the food that raised him,' read the motto. There was also a coffee-like drink called Postum. Dates came in a crate, one massive slab of compressed dates that had to be cut into smaller pieces and weighed for sale. But many other foods had to be measured out from sacks into tough blue bags. Mum helped by making Scotch eggs to be displayed in the shop window. We had a very heavy snowfall and my Dad was concerned about the weight of snow on his roof .We three went up to have a look. Dad opened the skylight in the attic and began to move the snow and then gave us all a fright when he climbed out on to the roof - there was only a simple rail over the gutter and it was quite precarious.

I can 'see' vividly the year, 1924, when I was given a bicycle. Up to then I had nothing much: a wooden hoop and a whip-top. This top was kept spinning on the pavement by whipping it. One day my lash sent the top over a hedge and through someone's window. That cost my father seven shillings and sixpence (£57.60 today). The cycle was my joy for years. There were few cars about then and I could ride anywhere in the quieter roads. In fact a friend who had a bike and I used to practise stunts. I learned to cycle sitting backwards on the handlebar and pedal with the opposite feet as it were. There would be no traffic coming. Of course, I fell off a few times. I bought a cyclometer and kept a record of my longer rides. I wrote the mileage in pencil on the back wall of the house.

Another strong memory is that of reading. At first, my mother used to go to the Small Heath branch of the Birmingham City Libraries. In the 1920s it was still run like a post office. You chose books over a counter. Thus books just returned soon went out again. Mum thought I would like adventure stories by Henry or Westerman. I did not. I much preferred the school stories of Greyfriars. Years later the library was converted to 'open access' and I spent many hours there browsing. One of the great mysteries of the mind is that I can 'see' all these events just as though they happened yesterday.

A SUFFOLK LAD BORN AND BRED

by John White

I was born in October, 1939, in the small Suffolk village of Kirton, a traditional English place with a church, a pub, a forge and a village green. My first memory is of being in a pram under the stairs as an air raid took place in 1940. 'We'll be alright, John', my mother said. Eventually, though, I was evacuated in 1942 to my father's family at Helston in Cornwall.

My father, Joseph, a mechanical engineer with the AMWD (Air Ministry Works Directorate) was transferred in 1944 to RAF Halton, Bucks. We lived in two terraced houses in Clay Lane, Wendover, with the toilet at the bottom of the back garden. There was rationing and this was an era of the 'make do and mend' culture - no car, a strong community spirit, and friends to roam around with all day with no dangers obvious. I started Wendover C of E School (all age then) in September 1944. My first teacher was Miss Marshall – I spent my first morning sitting on her knee – it felt warm and safe – I liked school after that! Corporal punishment was severe, nit inspections, inkwells and blotting paper, 'Beacon' reading books, all teachers were 'Miss' and my first girlfriend was Sally Lupton, aged eight. My baby brother, Alan Robert, arrived in 1946 – an Aylesbury duck!

I failed the 11-plus scholarship twice in successive years – not surprising since I wasn't interested in education. I wanted to be out on the Chiltern Hills playing with my pals and 'seeking adventure.' When my good friend Bryan Price passed for Aylesbury Grammar School for Boys, as well as class swot Peter Dawes, the headmaster Mr HJ Figg-Edgington, MA, told the whole school assembly to stand and applaud them. Suddenly, I then realised that education was not an 'assault on the self' but something important. I knew I was just as good as Bryan Price – I often came third in the tests of the 37 children in my class.

Inevitably, there was a school bully, an Irish boy called Bosco Hemmings. I defended a young lad from our street who was being bullied by him and we had a fight on Wendover High Street in front of the clock tower. I took my spectacles off and pushed Master Hemmings who fell over and hit his mouth on the kerb. What a deep cut it made and it poured with blood. I learned to stand up to bullies. Another classroom incident came when the pretty Penelope Widdowson sat in front of me in Miss Jones' class. She had long blonde hair and seemed to take delight in flicking her hair back over my maths page. I told her: 'If you do that again, I'll put your hair into the ink well.' She did - and I did. Ink went all over her blouse and I was sent to see the head who wouldn't listen to my side of the story and he caned me six times on both hands. From that episode I learned there are always two sides to any situation. I also wondered about fair play for all during these times. For instance, why were girls called by their Christian names and boys by their surnames?

The only holiday we ever went on was the Sunday school day trip to Margate. How we saved our threepenny bits and our pennies and how we looked forward to that special day at the seaside. Summer holidays at home seemed to involve long sunny days with a haversack, into which went a bottle of water and some jam sandwiches. We climbed trees, made dens, damned streams, fished for sticklebacks, scrumped orchards, made rafts, swam in the reservoir, and played football with coats as goal posts. I always felt safe with my mates.

I was baptised at Kirton C of E Church, Suffolk, by Rev WJS Wier in March 1940 and when our family moved to Wendover, I attended the Methodist church for morning service and Sunday school in the afternoon. At Nantwich I attended the Primitive Methodist chapel in Welsh Row. The minister was a significant man, Rev William Killcross, who suggested that I become a teacher. The Sunday school superintendent was Miss Phyllis Wilson, who took my first Sunday school class in 1956. I was accepted into the family of Methodism in 1958 and have always believed that 'my Christian belief is my foundation'.

I have always loved sports of all kinds – with 'average' ability. I represented schools at soccer, rugby, cricket, badminton, and tennis in every year of my education. I learned to enjoy the victories, but realised that the taking part is important, too. When my father was transferred to RAF Ballykelly, County Londonderry, Northern Ireland I was given a second chance vis a vis my education. I'd received a 'kick up the backside' by failing the 11+ scholarships in Wendover and I now realised that I had to take the whole concept a lot more seriously. I was subsequently successful in the 13-plus 'transfer' exam and interview at Limavady Grammar School. I made wonderful friends there: John Mullin, Desmond McCurry and Martin McCurry who were well-motivated and marvellous teachers. I passed the NI Junior School Certificate in 1955 with a distinction in Latin and five credits.

When my father was transferred to RAF Hack Green, near Nantwich in 1956, we moved to Queens Drive, just off Welsh Row and I went to Nantwich and Acton County Grammar School. I eventually passed seven 'O' levels. Again I had wonderful friends in Alan Hobson and Lawrence Whittaker and we have reunions every year. My secondary education ended in July 1958 and I started a two-year teacher training course at the Alsager Training College, in September 1958. Therefore the 'taught' soon became the 'teacher', with 'Doce ut Discas' (teach that you may learn) as its motto. One philosophy I've clung to: do as you would be done by. That has held me in good stead throughout my life.

MOTHER'S CLOSE CALL

by Janice Whitmore

I was a war baby and, as my Dad served in the Royal Marines, we had moved back in with grandparents so that Grandma could care for me while my mother did war work. Mum worked for the Co-op grocery stores and then at the new Rolls-Royce factory in Crewe. She was employed at Rolls-Royce when it was bombed in a terrible incident on the Sunday afternoon of December 29, 1940. Seventeen people were killed and hundreds injured. Fortunately she had been on the night shift the night before so was not on the site at the time. I dread to think what might have been, though. I've heard that up to 10,000 local people were employed at the Pym's Lane works and that a fifth of them were women. They made thousands of the Merlin engines used in our warplanes such as the Spitfire and the Lancaster bomber.

I have a vague memory of being carried into the Anderson shelter in my Grandma's back garden during these raids. It was equipped with a little camp bed for me and had an oil lamp in it, or it may have been an oil heater. Even now the smell of an oil lamp is very evocative of that time.

MR BLACK MARKET I PRESUME

by Janice Whitson

I was born in South Wales, towards the end of the Second World War. When I was young my parents and I lived with my grandmother in a small, terraced cottage. We had no bathroom, just an outside toilet in the back yard. Fortunately, it was only a short walk in the winter.

We had a long front garden and my father was very proud of his flowers and vegetables. Once, I remember him getting really cross when sheep came down from the moor and ate some of the produce - someone had left the gate open. We lived in a suburb of a large, industrial town. This was really a village with its own identity. Everyone knew most people and doors could be left unlocked with no fear of intruders.

There was one main street with small shops. We had two butchers' shops. One had the appropriate name of VEAL. There was a chemist, grocers and greengrocers. The grocer was referred to as Jones Black Market. When I was small, I thought his name really was Mr Black Market.

I began school life in the local primary school. I remember a huge sandpit in one room. We walked to school through a small park, which everyone called the Welfare ground. As well as swings for the children there were tennis courts, a bowling green and a snooker hall. We were banned from going near the snooker hall.

After the 11-plus, I moved to the grammar school. We were able to walk to school along the old dram road where they hauled limestone to Ebbw Vale blast furnaces. The school was opposite the terminus for the miners' train from the colliery. There was no station, the miners just climbed down from the carriages onto the track and over the fence. The train always arrived as we were leaving school in the afternoon. It must have seemed very strange seeing schoolchildren and miners walking home together. Many of the men were fathers of my friends.

Although there were pit baths, I can still remember the pit grime on the men. My father worked in the steelworks in a reserved occupation. Every year some of the staff performed a pantomime for the children of the workers. This was a first class show with a professional director and we looked forward to this with great excitement.

The churches and chapels played a big part in our lives. In our village there was one Church in Wales, which was the Anglican church, and seven chapels. There were two Congregational chapels. One was for English speakers and the other for Welsh speakers. Welsh was spoken by people from West Wales who had settled in the area after finding work in the valley, but most people spoke English and this was the language most used in everyday life.

Every Whitsun Monday we had the Church Walks, where members from each church paraded through the village singing. We practised our marching hymn for weeks beforehand. On the day we dressed in our best clothes and walked from chapel up the hill through the village and back again. The boys made peashooters and aimed them at other passing churches. Afterwards we returned to our chapel for tea and sports. Every chapel had a Sunday school and each year we had the Sunday school anniversary. I dreaded this as we were expected to recite or sing something. However, a few weeks later we were rewarded with an outing to the seaside. This was a very exciting day and seemed to make everything worthwhile.

I remember going on the bus to Abergavenny. This was a hazardous journey on very steep, narrow roads. Everyone gave a sigh of relief when we had safely negotiated the sharp bend by the Griffin pub. Lower down the hill, we passed another dangerous corner and I remember an old man in an Army coat who directed the traffic. He was made a Knight of the Road by a national newspaper.

My paternal grandmother lived in the Rhondda Valley and we visited her each Easter. We didn't own a car so it was a journey involving seven buses – now it takes 40 minutes by car!

189

After my grandmother died we moved to a bigger house. It was wonderful as it had a bathroom and an indoor toilet. I had a very happy childhood with a loving family. Although the area has changed (in many cases, beyond recognition) I have very affectionate memories of the people and places of my youth.

Here are some of the games we loved to play: marbles, hide and seek, Lucy Locket, squeak piggy squeak, blind man's buff, tag, what time is it Mr Wolf? the farmer's in his den and, of course, hop scotch and skipping.

LIFE ON THE OCEAN WAVE

by Peter Winby

I was at technical school thinking about going in the army when one of the teachers asked me if I'd considered the merchant navy. 'You have to go to Liverpool to be graded,' he told me. 'Then you can write to the navy company to see about getting a job as a navy officer.'

Attracted by the idea, I did as he instructed and got graded at Mersey Chambers. When I got back on the train home I looked at the paper and found that I'd been graded as class three which was not good enough for the navy. I was most annoyed that I'd seemingly forked out ten bob for a pointless exercise. Now my mother was a hairdresser and, naturally, had lot of customers. One of them had a son in the navy and I went to see him and he told me not to worry about the grading but to go to the library and get the addresses of several shipping companies and to write to several of them.

I applied to six of them then waited impatiently for a reply. Several said I did not have the right qualifications but three companies did give me a chance. Out of the three, I picked the Harrison Shipping Line and in due course went for an interview at Liverpool's Toxteth docks. Now my dad used to be a lorry driver so he knew his way around and he simply told me to get off the train at Lime Street, go down to the Pier Head and then turn left along the Dock Road and to keep going and I'd eventually come to Toxteth Dock. He never told me quite how far it was and I ended up running to get there on time, just about making it.

Although I'd been in my best clothes and thought I'd looked the 'bees knees,' by the time I arrived I was windblown and disheveled. I was directed to the main office where I stood waiting to be told to sit down. The man behind the desk just got up, came towards me and got hold of my jacket and straightened my tie and then returned to his desk. 'Now you look like you might one day be an officer,' he said.

I was sent for a medical, then returned to the office and was offered a job to start in a fortnight. The date was 24th of March, 1955. The difference between the army and the merchant navy is that you have to buy your own uniform in the latter. There were some shops around the docks that sold uniforms as 'made to measure'. What they did was to take a jacket from one rack and if it did not fit they would just keep going till they found a jacket that did fit and they would do the same with the trousers and so you finished up with a 'made to measure' uniform. My first ship was an old sand boat or liberty ship. These were built in the USA for the Second World War and were only supposed to last the one voyage across the Atlantic. But the British put a band of steel riveted all around the ship and they went on for years.

My first trip was down the Manchester Ship Canal. I was surprised how long it took. I knew that, eventually, I was not going to be put on a steam ship as I had no experience of steam engines so I was waiting for a motor ship to come in that needed a junior engineer. The MV Herdsman came into port and I was sent to join her as a sixth engineer. She had been built on the Tyne at Newcastle in 1945 and did not have the best of gear. The main engine was a five cylinder Doxford engine, but it was the auxiliary engines that were the trouble. The shipping company could not wait for new marine generators so they bought new army generators which did not have a big enough oil sump. When the ship rolled, the generator lost its oil pressure and this made a lot of work for the engineer.

Within a couple of months I was off on the ocean waves, deep sea to South Africa. Our first port of call was Port Elizabeth after a voyage of almost a month without seeing sight of land or even another vessel which was quite an experience for a young lad. Needless to say, I did a lot of travelling.

SHUSH, IT'S THE ARCHERS

by Glenis Wood

I was born at my grandparents' three-bed semi-detached council house, 20, Birtwistle Road, Rudheath, near Northwich. This was a place I visited every weekend during my childhood. My grandparents had a garden where they grew flowers and vegetables and kept hens. I remember the joy of newly hatched chicks and the smell of boiling potato peelings which we used to feed them. I also remember a neighbour's bantam that used to chase me (and ONLY me) and peck my bottom!

The garden there was a joy because we lived in a two bedroom terrace house where I shared a bed with my two sisters. We had a cobbled area at the back servicing six houses with a bank of six outside toilets in a line which meant that sometimes it could tend to be quite a communal experience. One of my jobs was to cut the newspaper into squares, make a hole in the corner and thread through a piece of string. This would be our loo paper, hung on a nail on the whitewashed wall. Toilet tissue was a joy I would not experience until I was in my teens!

We had just a cold water tap while cooking and lighting was by gas. I remember the journeys to the shop to buy a replacement gas mantle and sometimes the return (after skipping all the way) with a delicate mantle in pieces. What trouble I was in!

Every Friday was bath night; a tin bath in front of the range in the back kitchen. We bathed in turn. Fortunately, as the youngest, I went first and had the luxury of the clean water. Poor Dad! Monday was washday. The water had to be boiled and put into the dolly tub with dolly blue. Dolly peg and posser hopefully cleaned the clothes. They were then rinsed and a hand mangle squeezed out the water, all back-breaking work. Tuesday was ironing day with flat irons heated on the hob. I used to iron the tea towels and handkerchiefs. Evenings were spent making rag rugs using a sack as the base. These were our 'carpets'.

Our family were avid followers of *The Archers* on the radio, so not a word could be spoken during the programme, likewise during the football results when the pools coupon was checked. The house I grew up in was condemned and would be judged not fit for human habitation today. It was not until I was 13, however, that we were re-housed. A modern council house with a bathroom, hot and cold running water and electricity. What joy!

I passed my 11-plus and went to grammar school and then on to teacher training college. I was the first in my family to go on to higher education. I married my husband, Geoff, in 1967. We had two children, Benjamin and Rebecca and this made our family complete. Geoff was a policeman and had many tales to tell. His first job as a young constable was at Chester Assizes where he was assigned to guard the infamous 'Moors Murderers', Myra Hindley and Ian Brady. He had to stand in a dock and protect them from any attacks! As a Scenes of Crime-Officer he had many notorious crimes to try to solve. Congleton's horrific 'Boarded Barn' murder in 1979, when two women were killed, was another case he worked on.

Our holidays were spent caravanning and on one trip abroad, we got our 15 minutes of fame when our car and caravan fell off the ferry into the dock at Calais. We had 42 very happy years together before, sadly, Geoff died in 2009. I must say I enjoyed my teaching career, but I decided to call it a day once history lessons began to include items and objects from my own childhood and the children asked me: 'Mrs Wood, were these things in use when you were alive?'

The U3A (University of the Third Age) is a nationwide network of learning and leisure groups which originated in France. Although it caters mainly for retired or semi-retired people it is open to anyone no longer in full-time employment with no age restriction. Members share their knowledge, skills and interests. Each branch is semi-autonomous but shares the same ethos.

The U3A is **not** a University in the conventional sense – there are no exams and no homework!
It is **not** just for education but also has many **sporting** and **leisure** activities.

There are over 340,000 members in branches all over the UK and there will probably be one near to you. It is more like a friendly club than a University and if you are feeling lonely with nothing much to do this could be just the place for you! But be warned - some groups are so popular there may be a waiting list.

Crewe & Nantwich U3A is one of the largest in North West England with over 1500 members and 102 different courses. As they are all run by our volunteers we are able to keep subscriptions to an easily affordable level.

We cater for a great range of interests with something for everyone. Here are just a few: Photography, Art & Architecture, Bridge, Badminton, Computing for beginners, Table Tennis, Snooker, Bowls (Indoor & Outdoor), Craft, Painting, Dancing (3 types), Walking, Wine Appreciation, Exercise, Yoga, Local History, Chess, Scrabble, Gardening, Genealogy, Play Reading and 5 Languages.

For more details and how you can join - see the following **websites**:
U3A National: www.u3a.org.uk/
Crewe & Nantwich U3A: www.creweandnantwich-u3a.org.uk/